The Issue at Hand

Essays on Buddhist
Mindfulness Practice

GIL FRONSDAL

Grateful acknowledgement is made to the following for permission to print:

A version of "Theravada—The Way of Liberation." Originally published in *The Complete Guide to Buddhist America*, edited by Don Morreale © 1988, 1998 by Don Morreale. Reprinted by arrangement with Shambhala Publications, Inc., Boston, www.shambhala.com.

Material in the essays "Brief Instructions for Sitting Meditation," "Brief Instructions for Loving-Kindness Meditation," "Metta," and "Fear." Adapted from work previously published in "Voices from Spirit Rock" © 1996 Spirit Rock Meditation Center.

A version of "The Body at the Center." Originally published in Inquiring Mind (Fall 1994, Vol. II, No. 1).

A version of "Mindfulness of Intentions." Originally published in the Spirit Rock Newsletter in an article titled "Mindfulness with an Attitude" (March-August 1999).

A version of "Questioning as Practice." Originally published in Tricycle Magazine (Winter 2000, Vol. X, No. 2).

Third Edition August 2005.
Fourth Printing.

Cover Art and Design by Stephen Browning © 2001

CONTENTS

ACKNOWLEDGEMENTS

Many people contributed to the making of this book and I am very thankful and appreciative of their generosity. The seeds for the book and so much other good fruit come from the many initiatives taken by Elizabeth Adler and Bernice LaMar in supporting our sitting group. They were the first to tape, transcribe and edit my talks and set the ground for more to follow. Allicin Rauzin offered more support than I can possibly enumerate. Her dedicated efforts laid down much of the foundation for what our meditation center is today. Her years of taping meant that many of the talks were available for transcribing. I am also deeply grateful to the years of taping done by Louis Mendelowitz. And I am very appreciative of his steady and reliable help and the way his quiet efforts have been a backbone for our ongoing gatherings. I also extend my thanks to Jennifer Lemas and Glen Ingram for their good work with taping the talks.

Over the years many people have transcribed my talks. For

this I extend my thanks to Terry Craven, Judy Windt, Cheryll Gasner, Andrea Fella, Nancy Van House, Rainbow, Ann Mallard, Melissa Saphir, and Marge Martus.

The idea for this book came from Cheryl Hylton and is just one example of the many creative ideas she has offered in support of our meditation community.

The biggest thanks and acknowledgement go to Nancy Van House and Andrea Fella for the countless hours they spent editing my talks and writings. Without their efforts, this book would never have been published. It has been a real privilege for me to work with them and I offer to each a bow. Barbara Gates helped edit some of the essays originally published in Inquiring Mind and Tricycle. Many thanks for her generosity, care and expertise.

Andrea Fella was also the general editor for this book. Her spirit of care and careful consideration is found throughout these pages.

Early drafts of the book were reviewed and commented on by Thanissaro Bhikkhu, Tamara Kan, David Milne, Denise Kaplan, and Stephen Browning. Many thanks!

And special thanks to Elena Silverman, who devoted her expertise and love to the layout and design of this book. Also, many thanks to Stephen Browning for his artwork and design of the cover.

And finally, but not least, I extend my deep gratitude to all the people who have practiced together with me over the past eleven years that I have been teaching in Palo Alto. Perhaps, with my role as teacher, some people don't realize that I am practicing with the community. I see our community more as a place for me to practice than for me to teach. As such, my gratitude for the opportunity to be part of this practice community is boundless. Also, I am very aware that my teaching arises in relationship to those who hear it. Whatever wisdom or helpful words are found in this book, they are not my own; but rather, they arise out of our collective efforts to touch the Dharma. However, whatever is not wise in these pages I will take credit for. As someone once said, "All wisdom is plagiarism, only foolishness is original."

—Gil Fronsdal, 2001

INTRODUCTION: THE ISSUE AT HAND

Once upon a time, long ago, people walked about barefoot. One day, the queen, walking across a rock field, cut her foot on a sharp stone. Annoyed, she called together her ministers and ordered the Queendom carpeted with leather. One wise minister stepped forward and suggested an easier way. "Rather than covering the entire realm, let's cover the soles of everyone's feet." The Queen agreed and that was the origin of shoes.

It seems silly to cover a kingdom with leather to protect our feet. In the same way, some of our strategies for living are attempts to cover over our world. A much more effective way of living is to learn to take care of our point of direct contact with the world.

In the teachings of the Buddha, mindfulness is what brings us to the point of contact. Mindfulness entails knowing what is happening in the present moment while it is happening. It is a training in how not to be lost in thoughts, opinions, and reactivity. It is also a training in how to see things as they really are, as opposed to seeing them through the often distorted lens of preconceived ideas and interpretations.

Like shoes, mindfulness protects us. But shoes can only protect us from our outer world, i.e., the ground. Mindfulness protects us from both our outer and inner worlds. We are protected from the outer world because we can see it more clearly. We are protected from both the outer and the inner worlds by being mindful and discerning in how we react. Mindfulness strengthens our ability to avoid harmful impulses and to act beneficially.

Training in mindfulness is thus a training in finding the point of contact. Another way of saying this is that it involves the search for "the issue at hand." I like this expression because the image of a hand suggests what can be touched, what can be directly seen and felt.

If we spend a lot of time anticipating the future, the issue at hand is not the future event, but rather what is tangible in the present—the immediate physical and mental experiences of worry or excitement. If we spend a lot of time in fantasy, the issue at hand might be the physical sensations of the boredom fueling the story making. If we are in an angry conversation, we won't find the issue at hand in rehashing past events or in dwelling on our judgements of the other person. Instead, we find it by grounding the conversation in what each person is feeling during the conversation. This does not mean we can't review the past, but it does mean we don't lose contact with ourselves and the other person.

The search for the issue at hand is the search for what is closest at hand, for what is directly seen, heard, smelt, tasted, felt, and cognized in the present. Sometimes what is closest at hand is how we are holding our direct experience. When I teach mindfulness to children, I hold a small bell in my hand. First I grasp it tightly and show them that when I hit the bell with the striker, it makes a dull thud. Then I balance the bell on my open hand, not grasping it at all. When I strike it this time, it rings beautifully.

When grasping is seen as being what is closest at hand, mindfulness attends carefully to the grasping. In doing so, one of the basic tasks of mindfulness is to help us to release our grasping. It is indeed possible to have our direct contact with ourselves and the world around us be characterized by the absence of grasping. The closed hand, the grasping hand, the resisting hand can all be relaxed. We can perhaps touch this earth of ours with the same gentleness and tenderness with which the Buddha reached down to touch the earth on the night of his enlightenment.

———

The book you are now holding in your hands is a compilation of essays and edited talks on the Buddhist practice of mindfulness. Many of these chapters started out as talks given to the Monday evening or Sunday morning sitting groups of our Insight Meditation Center of the Mid-Peninsula. A few of the chapters were written specifically for publication in Buddhist journals, magazines, or newsletters.

This book is an offering of the Dharma. Just as the point of going to a restaurant is not to read the menu, but rather to eat, so the point of a Dharma book is not found in just reading it or even in understanding it. My hope is that the teachings herein are an encouragement to study the issue at hand.

Just this is the path.
For purifying one's vision, there is no other.
Follow it
And you will bewilder Mara.
Follow it
And you will put an end to suffering.
—Dhammapada 274-275

THE FOUR NOBLE TRUTHS

On one occasion the Blessed One was dwelling at Kosambi in a grove of trees. Then the Blessed One took up a few leaves in his hand and addressed the bhikkhus thus: "What do you think, bhikkhus, which is more numerous: these few leaves that I have taken up in my hand or those in this grove of trees?"

"Venerable sir, the leaves that the Blessed One has taken up in his hand are few, but those in the grove of trees are numerous."

"So too, bhikkhus, the things I have directly known but have not taught you are more numerous, while the things I have taught you are few. And why, bhikkhus have I not taught those many things? Because they are unbeneficial, irrelevant to the fundamentals of the holy life...and do not lead to peace...."

Samyutta Nikaya V.437-438

As this *sutta* shows us, the Buddha taught only a very small portion of what he knew. Elsewhere, the Buddha said, "I teach one thing and one thing only, suffering and the end of suffering." This is one of the simplest definitions of Buddhist practice and speaks to our capacity to move from suffering to freedom from suffering. From this place, we can meet the world in a compassionate and receptive way.

Our tradition is very simple. Some people might feel it is poverty stricken because it just has a handful of leaves. It doesn't have all the leaves on all the trees in the grove. Some people may be dazzled trying to focus on the immensity of all the leaves. In the Theravada tradition the focus is on understanding suffering and how to become free of it, how to become happy. What we need to know to become free is actually very little.

In his first sermon, "Turning the Wheel of the Dharma," the Buddha taught about suffering and the end of suffering in the form of the Four Noble Truths. After more than 2500 years they have come to us as the core teachings of Buddhism. Almost all Buddhist traditions consider the Four Noble Truths to be very central teachings. Intellectually, they are easy to understand, but it is said that a deep understanding of the full impact of these Four Truths is possible only for someone whose liberation is fully mature.

When he formulated the teaching of the Four Noble Truths, the Buddha borrowed a medical model. At the time of the Buddha, doctors would recognize the problem, define its cause, formulate the prognosis for a cure, and then prescribe a course of action. The Buddha adopted this formulation when he stated the Four Noble Truths:

1. Suffering occurs.
2. The cause of suffering is craving.
3. The possibility for ending suffering exists.
4. The cessation of suffering can be attained through the Noble Eightfold Path.

I think it is significant that he chose to follow a medical model, because it avoids metaphysics. The religions of the world tend to be imbued with metaphysical or cosmological beliefs that followers are required to accept before the rest of the system can make sense. But the Buddha felt that metaphysical speculation was not beneficial in understanding liberation, the freedom from suffering. He avoided dogma. He offered practices and insights that we can verify for ourselves, rather than a doctrine to believe in. Indeed, part of the brilliance of the Four Noble Truths is that they offer a guide to the spiritual life without the need to adhere to any metaphysical beliefs.

The Truth of Suffering

The First Noble Truth simply says that suffering occurs. It does not say, "Life is suffering." That suffering occurs perhaps does not seem a particularly profound statement. Suffering comes with being human. Pain is a part of the human condition. We stub our toe, and it hurts. Our back goes out. Even the Buddha was subject to physical suffering; at times he declined to give a Dharma talk because of pain in his back. Emotional pain is inevitable if we are open to the world. When other people suffer around us, and we are open to it, we ourselves sometimes feel discomfort through our powers of empathy. Part of being human is to relate to and feel what is going on around us. However, pain is not the kind of suffering that the Buddha was trying to help us become free of.

In the context of the Four Noble Truths, we can distinguish between inevitable suffering and optional suffering. Optional suffering is created when we react to our experience—for example, through anger at the inevitable suffering of pain, or by clinging to joy. When we suffer from physical pain or illness, we can become self-judgmental: "What did I do wrong to have this thing happen to *me*?" We attack ourselves, or we blame others. Or we become angry, sad, or depressed about the suffering in the world. Optional suffering is added when we react with aversion or clinging, justification or condemnation. These reactions add complications and suffering to our lives. It is possible to experience the inevitable pain of life in a straightforward, uncomplicated way. If pain is inevitable, life is a lot easier if we don't resist it.

So, the teaching of the Four Noble Truths does not promise relief from the inevitable suffering that arises out of being human. The suffering addressed by the Four Noble Truths is the suffering or stress that arises from the way we choose to relate to our experience. When we cling, it is painful. When we try to hold our experience at a distance, to push it away, that too is painful. We cling to or push away from our experience in an infinite variety of ways.

The way to practice with the Four Noble Truths is to become very interested in our suffering. Ancient texts say that no one comes to the Buddhist path except through suffering. From a Buddhist perspective, the recognition of suffering is sacred; it is worthy of respect. We need to study our suffering, to get to know it well in the same way that we hope our doctors take our illnesses seriously. If suffering is powerful in our lives, we have a strong motivation to study it.

But not all suffering is monumental. What we can learn from more subtle suffering helps us to understand the deeper suffering of our lives. So it is also important to study minor suffering in our lives: our frustration with a traffic jam, or irritation toward co-workers.

We can study our suffering by attending to where and how we cling. The Buddha enumerated four kinds of clinging to help us understand our suffering and what we suffer about. The one Westerners might consider easiest to let go of is grasping to spiritual practices and ethics. We may grasp our practice because we cling to the hope of freedom from suffering. We may grasp the rules of spiritual practice, thinking that all that is required of us is simply to follow the rules. Or we might use our practice to create a spiritual identity. We may grasp our practice to run away from life, or we may grasp precepts and ethics for security. Sometimes, we feel like the Buddhist path is so wonderful that we become attached to getting others to practice also. Clinging to spiritual practice causes suffering for ourselves and discomfort for others.

The second type of clinging is grasping to views. This includes all opinions, stories or judgements that we hold on to. These can have a powerful grip on us and on our perception of the world around us. Believing in views and basing our actions on them is something that few of us question. Many of our emotions arise out of views; even our sense of self can be constructed from them.

A classic example that illustrates how views create emotions is how you might react if someone misses an appointment with you. You had a date, you are waiting on a street corner in the cold, and the person doesn't show up. This is all that is actually happening.

To those facts, we often add a story: the person doesn't respect me. With that evaluation, anger arises. The anger doesn't arise because we are standing on a street corner and someone hasn't shown up. The anger arises because we are fixated on the story, which may or may not be true. The person could have had an accident and be in the emergency room. We need to know what our interpretations or suppositions are and then hold them lightly, prepared for the possibility that they might not be true. Or if they prove true, we then need to know how to act wisely without clinging even to the truth.

The third form of clinging is grasping to a sense of self. We construct an identity and hold on to it. The construction of an identity or self-definition is actually the construction of a view. It is the "story of me," and we attach to it rather than just letting things be as they are. Maintaining and defending a self-image can be a lot of work. It can fuel a lot of self-conscious pre-occupation with how we speak, dress, and behave. We evaluate everything according to how it relates to ourselves, causing ourselves endless suffering.

The fourth type of clinging is grasping to sensual pleasure, which includes aversion to discomfort. In the Buddhist texts, this is the first in the list of things that we cling to; I put it last because it sometimes puts people off. Sensual pleasure itself is not the problem; our lives will bring us many sensual pleasures. The problem is that we cling to them. William Blake expresses this beautifully:

> *He who binds to himself a joy*
> *Does the wingèd life destroy.*
> *But he who kisses the joy as it flies*
> *Lives in eternity's sunrise.*

Attachment to sense pleasures is so pervasive in us that many of us feel something is wrong when things are unpleasant. But unpleasant sensations are just unpleasant sensations until we add a story to them. Confusing pleasure with happiness is a powerful fuel for the attachment to pleasure. An important part of Buddhist spiritual practice is discovering a happiness not connected to objects of desire and pleasure. With this discovery, the seductive enchantment of sensual pleasure begins to lessen.

The Truth of the Cause of Suffering

The word *dukkha*, which we translate as suffering, is closely connected to the word *sukha*, which means happiness. They both have the same root: *-kha*, which means, etymologically, the hub of a wheel. *Du-* means "bad", while *su-* means "good". So etymologically, *dukkha* means "a wheel out of kilter", or "a wheel off center."

The Second Noble Truth states that what brings us off center, what causes our suffering, is craving. In Pali, the word is *tanha*, which literally means thirst. It is sometimes translated as desire but this tends to suggest that all desires are a problem. What causes suffering is desire (or aversion) that is driven, compulsive. Craving means both being driven toward experiences and objects, as well as feeling compelled to push them away. Whether craving is subtle or gross, if we aren't mindful, we won't be aware of how it contributes to our suffering.

Part of the reason that Buddhism puts a tremendous focus on the present moment is that suffering *only* occurs in the present moment. In addition, the craving, the *cause* of that suffering, occurs only in the present moment. Even when the conditions for suffering occurred in the past, the thought or memory of those conditions is occurring in the present. We emphasize the present moment in our practice as an attempt to understand clearly how craving functions in the present moment. In the present moment we can find both the cause and the relief from our suffering.

So, quite simply, the present moment is the place where we will understand the Four Noble Truths. As we practice, first we try to stabilize ourselves in the present moment. We settle into our body, listen to sounds, or feel the sensations of breathing. Once we are in the present moment, we can begin exploring our experience: what we are driven toward, what we push away, how we create our suffering.

The Truth of the Cessation of Suffering

The Third Noble Truth expresses the possibility of liberation, of the cessation of suffering. When we see our suffering and understand clearly how it arises out of craving, we know that freedom from suffering is possible when craving is released.

The word *nibbana* or *nirvana* refers to freedom from suffering. While the Theravada tradition sometimes describes *nibbana* as a great happiness or peace, more often it has been defined as resulting from the complete absence of clinging or craving. One reason for this negative definition is that *nibbana* is so radically different from what can be described through language that it is best not to try. Another reason is so that the goal of Buddhist practice is not obscured with metaphysical speculations about the nature of the goal.

Still another reason for the negative definition of *nibbana* is to avoid confusing it with any particular states of being. We easily become attached to states such as calm, peace, joy, clarity, or radiant light—states that sometime arise during meditation practice, but which are not its goal. We may believe that we need to attain them if we are to realize the Third Noble Truth. But if we remember non-clinging is the means to release, then we will be less inclined to cling to any state. Don't cling to your happiness. Don't cling to your sadness. Don't cling to any attainment.

The Truth of the Path Leading to the Cessation of Suffering

Letting go of all of our clinging is not easy. Developing the understanding, compassion, and mindfulness to see well enough to let go of our suffering is quite difficult. The Fourth Noble Truth is pragmatic; it describes, in eight steps, the path that leads to freedom from suffering. The Noble Eightfold Path gives us the steps that help us to create the conditions that make spiritual maturity possible. They are:

1. Right Understanding
2. Right Intention
3. Right Speech
4. Right Action
5. Right Livelihood
6. Right Effort
7. Right Mindfulness
8. Right Concentration

Sometimes this list is taught sequentially. A practitioner develops them in order, first clarifying his or her understanding and intention in order to stay off roads tangential to the simple path of the Four Noble Truths, then setting in order his or her behavior in the world so that it can support the inner development of Right Effort, Right Mindfulness, and Right Concentration. In the sequential approach, a practitioner does not complete each step before moving on to the next. Rather, the practice follows a spiral path in which one continually returns to the beginning, each time with greater depth.

Sometimes the list is not taught as a path to be developed sequentially. Rather the eight steps are presented as eight aspects of the path, which are developed together. They are mutually supportive, each nourishing the others. The list is comprehensive; it shows us how we can bring the full range of our lives onto the path of practice. We can see this when these eight are categorized with the divisions of body, speech and mind. Right Action and Livelihood pertain to our bodily activities, Right Speech to our verbal ones, and the remainder to the domain of the mind and heart.

Sometimes the Eightfold Path is divided into the three categories of ethics, inner practices, and insight (*sila, samadhi,* and *pañña*). In this case, Right Speech, Right Action, and Right Livelihood, as aspects of ethics, are taught as the beginning of the path. Following the development of ethics, the inner practices of effort, mindfulness and concentration lead to the development of insight or wisdom.

The Eightfold path offers a rich world of practice. Studying and becoming familiar with all eight is well worth the time and effort.

Of the Eight, the *Vipassana* tradition puts particular emphasis on mindfulness. In part, this is because when the mindfulness practice is thorough, the other aspects of the Eightfold Path follow in its wake.

Mindfulness is also the key element for the transformation of liberation. Mindfulness practice is the vehicle for realizing the Four Noble Truths. In mindfulness practice, we learn how to pay attention in the present moment so that when suffering arises we're able to notice it. We can take an interest in it instead of running away from it. We can learn how to be comfortable with suffering, so that we don't act inappropriately because of our discomfort. Then we can begin understanding its roots, and let go of the clinging.

All of the Buddha's teachings are an elaboration of the Four Noble Truths. By understanding this handful of leaves a spiritual life can be straightforward and practical. We can all experience the great joy and peace that comes from the freedom from clinging.

Why the laughter, what the joy
  When flames are ever burning?
Surrounded by darkness
  Shouldn't you seek for light?

—*Dhammapada 146*

INTOLERANCE TO SUFFERING

Buddhism is often considered a religion of tolerance. In many ways it is. But a particular kind of intolerance develops as we practice: intolerance to suffering. I use the word "intolerance" to be deliberately provocative, to encourage you to reflect on suffering and the issues surrounding it.

Taking suffering seriously is an important element of Buddhist practice. To ignore it is to miss a powerful opportunity. Intolerance to suffering motivated the Buddha to find liberation from it. Suffering, a feeling of dissatisfaction with life, motivates people to engage in spiritual practice. The Buddha's challenge is for us to become free of our suffering.

People are often quite tolerant of their suffering, particularly of the subtle suffering in everyday activities. For example, we may not pay attention to the subtle tension in the way we drive: going a little faster than is comfortable, judging other drivers, or perhaps being anxious about our destination. Such minor stress tends to build over time, affecting our overall mood.

People also tolerate larger suffering. For example, we may be afraid that addressing certain issues in our relationships will cause even more suffering, so we choose not to. Or we may passively tolerate such existential anxiety as the fear of death, never really looking into it deeply, never freeing ourselves of its grip on our life.

We have many ways of tolerating suffering, and many reasons for doing so. We may fear the consequences of facing our suffering. We may become numb to it, or turn away from it. We can intentionally deny the existence of something that is quite uncomfortable.

We may also tolerate our suffering because of ambition or desire. Or we may be willing to tolerate some suffering to achieve what we perceive is a greater good. Sometimes this tolerance is a necessary component of life. To graduate from college, for example, many of us tolerated unpleasant situations. We were willing to put up with the discomfort because of the value of education.

But such tradeoffs are not always worthwhile. When we consider our deepest values, we may find that what we are pursuing is not really worth it. For example, financial wealth may not be worth the years of stress needed to achieve it.

Major crises and personal tragedies can be very difficult to deal with, but they can be easier if we have had experience with smaller issues. The subtle suffering in our lives—such as in the way we drive, or talk to co-workers—may seem unimportant. But if we attend to the small ways that we suffer, we create a context of greater ease, peace, and responsibility, which can make it easier to deal with the bigger difficulties when they arise.

Being intolerant of suffering, in the Buddhist sense, does not mean that we reject it or fight against it. It means that we stop and look at it, not morbidly, but rather because we have faith in the possibility of living a joyful and peaceful life, if we can understand our sufferings.

In Buddhist practice, we investigate the nature of suffering. One of the first things we may notice is our relationship to it. We may discover how we tolerate, avoid or accept suffering in unhealthy ways.

We may notice our aversion to suffering. Trying to push something out of the heart is another form of suffering. Aversion to suffering creates even more suffering.

We may also notice how suffering functions in our lives. We might be using it as proof of or justification for inappropriate judgements about ourselves: e.g., that we are blameworthy, inadequate, or incapable. Identifying strongly with our suffering can become our orientation to the world. Occasionally people hang on to the identity "I'm a victim," and want to be treated by others as a victim. We can use our suffering to get other people to respond to us in ways that may not be healthy.

However, being willing to investigate suffering and to look at it closely and non-reactively changes our relationship to it. We bring a healthy part of our psyche to the experience of suffering. Instead of being wrapped up in our suffering, lost in aversion to it, or shut off from it, we simply ask: "What is this?" This movement toward a different relationship with our suffering is an important aspect of Buddhist practice.

Meditation practice helps us develop concentration. When we develop concentration on something as simple as the breath, we counter the force of our attachments with the strength of our concentration. Concentration often creates a sense of calm, ease, and even joy that in turn begins to change our relationship to suffering. But concentration is only a part of mindfulness practice. Mindfulness strengthens our ability to look honestly and steadily at the sources of our suffering. It helps us to see that the roots of our suffering are actually in the present moment. The conditions that gave birth to suffering may be in the past, and understanding past conditions can be very helpful. But suffering occurs in the present moment, and is actually held in place by craving, aversion or fear that are also occurring in the present. If we can release the holding, suffering loosens. Mindfulness joined with concentration allows us to see the moment-to-moment holding at the heart of our suffering.

Intolerance to suffering may co-exist with joy. Certainly not joy in the suffering itself, but the joy of bringing our practice to bear on it. As we become intolerant of our suffering and face it honestly, we begin to see the possibility of living a joyful and peaceful life.

Attentive among the inattentive,
  Wide awake among the sleeping.
The wise one advances
  As a swift horse leaves behind a weak one
                                  —Dhammapada 29

THE PRACTICE OF MINDFULNESS

In the *Mahaparinibbana Sutta*, the scripture that records the Buddha's last teachings, the Buddha summarizes what he discovered with his awakening and what he taught during his 45 years as a teacher. Significantly, he does not recount a set of doctrines or a belief system, but rather gives a list of practices and spiritual qualities that grow with a spiritual life. By teaching practices instead of "truths," the Buddha offered methods to help us uncover our potential for peaceful, compassionate and liberated lives. In a sense, Buddhist practice is concerned with discovering what is truest for each of us in our own hearts and bodies rather than what tradition, scriptures or teachers may tell us is true.

Insight meditation, or *Vipassana*, is one of the central teachings of the Buddha. It has continued as a living practice for 2500 years. At the heart of insight meditation is the practice of mindfulness, the cultivation of clear, stable and nonjudgmental awareness. While mindfulness practice can be highly effective in helping bring calm and clarity to the pressures of daily life, it is also a spiritual path that gradually dissolves the barriers to the full development of our wisdom, compassion and freedom.

The word *Vipassana* literally means "clear seeing." Cultivating our capacity to see clearly is the foundation for learning how to be present for things as they are, as they arise. It is learning to see without the filters of bias, judgement, projection, or emotional reactions. It also entails developing the trust and inner strength that allow us to be with things as they are instead of how we wish they could be. Mindfulness practice does not involve *trying* to change who we are, instead it is a practice of seeing clearly who we are, of seeing what is happening as it unfolds, without interference. In the process, even without trying, we can be transformed.

Mindfulness relies on an important characteristic of awareness: awareness by itself does not judge, resist, or cling to anything. By focusing on simply being aware, we learn to disentangle ourselves from our habitual reactions and begin to have a friendlier and more compassionate relationship with our experience, with ourselves, and with others.

However, awareness is often confused with self-consciousness, in which we judge what we are experiencing against our opinions and image of ourselves.

For instance, if we get angry during a period of meditation, a self-conscious response might be "Shoot! I'm angry again! I hate myself for always being so angry." With mindfulness practice we cultivate an awareness that recognizes anger's presence without judging it—we would be mindful that "There is anger."

If we see a beautiful flower, with awareness we simply appreciate the flower. A self-conscious response might be "That's a beautiful flower, and I want it for myself so people will know I have good taste and they will admire me."

A foundation stone of Buddhist practice and teaching is a great appreciation for the present. This includes the recognition that the most wonderful things that we have in life happen only if we are in the present moment. For friendship, joy, generosity, compassion, and appreciation of beauty to arise, we have to allow ourselves the time and the presence to be aware.

Appreciating the present moment involves learning that the present moment is trustable if we are present for it. If we can be wholeheartedly mindful and non-reactive to what is going on in the present, then we will learn to respond appropriately.

Having appreciation and trust is not always easy. Part of Buddhist practice is to discover what prevents us from trusting and appreciating the present moment. What is our actual frustration, what is our resistance, what is our suffering, what is our mistrust? When these are operating, the job of mindfulness is to clearly recognize them and then to hold them non-judgmentally with our awareness.

Buddhist teachings suggest that when we find the thing that keeps us from appreciating the present, the thing that keeps us from trusting, the very thing that causes us suffering, it is a gate to freedom, to awakening. We learn to live with openness and trust rather than with a self-image and all the self-criticism, aversion and pride that can come with it. In mindfulness practice, none of our humanity is denied. We are discovering a way to be present to everything—our full humanity—so everything becomes a gate to freedom, to compassion and to ourselves.

Like a fish out of water,
Thrown on high ground,
This mind thrashes about
Trying to escape Mara's command.

—Dhammapada 34

HOW MINDFULNESS WORKS
WHEN IT DOESN'T WORK

In practicing mindfulness, it can be helpful to remember that the practice works even when it doesn't seem to work. Perhaps this is explained best through an analogy.

Consider a mountain stream where the water is quite clear, and seems placid and still. But if you place a stick into the water, a small wake around the stick shows that in fact the water is flowing. The stick becomes a reference point that helps us notice the movement of the water.

Similarly, the practice of mindfulness is a reference point for noticing aspects of our lives that we may have missed. This is especially true for mindfulness of breathing. In trying to stay present for the breath, you may become aware of the concerns and the momentum of the mind that pull the attention away from the breath. If you can remain with the breath, then obviously mindfulness of breathing is working. However, if your attempt to stay with the breath results in increased awareness of what pulls you away from the breath, then the practice is also working.

Without the reference of mindfulness practice, it is quite easy to remain unaware of the preoccupations, tensions, and momentum operating in your life. For example, if you are busily doing many things, the concern for getting things done can blind you to the tension building in the body and mind. Only by stopping to be mindful may you become aware of the tensions and feelings that are present.

Sometimes your attempt to be with the breath is the only way that you see the speed at which the mind is racing. Riding on a train, if you focus on the mountains in the distance, you might not notice the speed of the train. However, if you bring your attention closer, the rapidly appearing and disappearing telephone poles next to the tracks reveal the train's speed. Even when you have trouble staying with the breath, your continued effort to come back to the breath can highlight what might otherwise be unnoticed, i.e., the rapid momentum of the mind. In fact, the faster our thinking and the greater the preoccupation, the greater the need for something close by like the breath to help bring an awareness of what is going on. That awareness, in turn, often brings some freedom from the preoccupation.

When staying with the breath during meditation is difficult, we can easily get discouraged. However, that difficulty is an opportunity to become more aware of the forces of mind and the feelings causing the distractions. Remember, if we learn from what is going on, regardless of what is happening, the practice is working, even when it seems not to be working, when we aren't able to stay with the breath.

Even when it is relatively easy to stay with the breath, mindfulness of the breathing can still function as an important reference point. In this case it may not be a reference point for the strong forces of distraction, but rather for subtler thoughts and feelings that may lie close to the root of our concerns and motivations. Don't pursue those thoughts or feelings. Simply be aware of their presence while continuing to develop the meditation on the breath, so that the breath can become an even more refined reference point. When we are settled on the breath, the heart becomes clear, peaceful, and still like a mountain pool. Then we can see all the way to the bottom.

Through effort, attention,
    Restraint and self-control,
The wise person can become an island
    No flood will overwhelm.

—Dhammapada 25

THE STORMS OF SPIRITUAL LIFE

Expecting Buddhist practice to entail only joy and ease is naive. More realistic is to expect both joy and sorrow, ease and struggle. If the practice is to engage with our full life, then inevitably we will practice in times of crisis, loss, or painful self-confrontation. Certainly it would be nice to negotiate these times with calm, grace and wisdom. However, if we are hard on ourselves for not doing so, we only add to our suffering and hinder the growth of compassion.

Evaluating our spiritual practice by the presence of joy and ease is often myopic; it overlooks the range of other personal qualities that we need to develop. An analogy may illustrate this:

Imagine two people setting out to cross a large lake, each in a small rowboat. The first sets out on a clear day with the lake surface as still and flat as a mirror, a gentle breeze and a steady current pushing the boat from behind. Each time the oars are dipped into the water, the boat shoots across the lake. Rowing is easy and delightful. Quickly the rower reaches the far side of the lake. She may congratulate herself for being quite skilled.

The second rower heads out across the same lake during a great storm. Powerful winds, currents, and waves move in the direction opposite the boat. With each pull of the oars, the boat barely moves forward, only to lose most of the distance gained when the oars are raised out of the water for the next pull. After much effort she makes it to the far side of the lake. This rower may feel discouraged at her lack of skill.

Probably most people would prefer to be the first rower. However, the second rower is the one who has become stronger from the exertion and is thereby better prepared for future challenges.

I have known meditators who have congratulated themselves for their meditative proficiency when practice has been easy. And I have known meditators filled with doubt and self-condemnation when the practice has been stormy. Practicing with our best effort during periods of crisis and personal struggle may not bring about spiritual highs. It may, however, bring something more important: a strengthening of the inner qualities that sustain a spiritual life for the long term: mindfulness, persistence, courage, compassion, humility, renunciation, discipline, concentration, faith, acceptance, and kindness.

For Buddhist practice, one of the most important inner capacities to develop is awareness of intention. Our intention is like a muscle; following through on our intention to practice—to be mindful and compassionate—during times of difficulty is an important way of strengthening it. The beauty of this is that, even if our efforts are clumsy or if we don't accomplish a particular task, the "intention muscle" has still been strengthened every time we use it, especially if it is being nourished by faith and clear comprehension. As our core motivations become stronger and we develop more confidence and appreciation in them, they become a resource and refuge in times of difficulty.

Meditators all too often measure their practice by their "meditative experiences." While a range of such potential experiences can play an important role in Buddhist spirituality, day-to-day practice is more focused on developing our inner faculties and strengths. This includes cultivating awareness and investigation in all circumstances, whether the weather is clear or stormy. A wealth of inner strength follows in the wake of mindfulness and persistence. Such strength is often accompanied by feelings of calm and joy; but, more important, it allows us to remain awake and free under conditions of both joy and sorrow.

Whatever a mother, father
Or other relative may do,
Far better is the benefit
From one's own rightly directed mind.
—*Dhammapada 43*

HEARTFELT PRACTICE

The English word "mindfulness" is the usual translation for the Pali word *sati*. Most generally, *sati* means to hold something in awareness. When the Chinese translated Indian Buddhist terms into Chinese characters, *sati* became a character with two halves: the top half is the character for " the present moment" and the bottom half is the character for "heart." The combination suggests that mindfulness is connected to the heart, to being "heartfelt in the present moment." It points to the possibility of holding our experience in our hearts, to having an accepting, soft, and spacious awareness toward whatever is occurring.

At times, mindfulness practice can feel a bit dry. It can seem to involve a detached, objective or unfeeling attitude toward our experience in the present moment. However, such an attitude arises when mindfulness is confused with subtle fear, distance, resistance, or judgement. Luckily, the mindfulness practice is self-correcting: the continual effort to notice what is actually going on in the present will in due time reveal the subtle tension that underlies a detached attitude. If we can clearly recognize the dryness of practice, it can be a signal that helps us re-establish a softer, more tender presence. Or alternatively it can be an indication that we need to hold the very dryness with soft acceptance.

Many of us have hearts that are encrusted with anxieties, fears, aversions, sorrows, and an array of defensive armor. The non-reactive and accepting awareness of mindfulness will help to dissolve these crusts. The practice has a cyclic quality; it is self-reinforcing. At first, the practice will allow us to let go of a small amount of defensiveness. That release allows a corresponding amount of openness and tender-heartedness to show itself. This process encourages us to drop even more armor. Slowly, a greater sense of heartfeltness supports the further development of mindfulness.

As our neurotic thought patterns drop away, layers of judgment and resistance atrophy, and the need to define our selves through hard-held identities relaxes. As this happens, the natural goodness of the heart shines by itself.

The impulses to be aware, happy, compassionate, and free, all come from the goodness of our hearts. As we connect to these intentions and allow them to motivate our mindfulness practice, the practice becomes heartfelt.

The Thai meditation master Ajahn Chah said that everything occurs within the heart. In mindfulness practice, we let our heart hold whatever arises within itself.

All we experience is preceded by mind,
  Led by mind, made by mind.
Speak or act with a corrupted mind
  And suffering follows
As the wagon wheel follows the hoof of the ox.
All we experience is preceded by mind,
  Led by mind, made by mind.
Speak or act with a peaceful mind
  And happiness follows
Like a shadow that never leaves.

—Dhammapada 1-2.

KARMA

Central to Buddhist spiritual practice is a deep appreciation of the present moment and the possibilities that exist in the present for waking up and being free of suffering. The present is the only place our creativity exists. The Buddhist notion of karma is closely tied to that creativity.

The concept of karma is not some idea about past lives; nor is it a law of predetermination. If you believe that your happiness is predetermined, it leaves no space for you to affect your happiness and your suffering. Spiritual practice includes choice. The Buddha stressed that if you have too strict an idea of karma, there is no room for choice.

The Buddha said, "What I call karma is intention." In other words, the teaching of karma is about the intentional choices we make in the present. The present moment is to be appreciated mindfully and relaxed into, as we do in meditation. But it is also where we choose how to step forward into the next moment. The more clearly we see the choice, the greater the freedom and creativity we have in making it.

The present moment is partly the result of our choices in the past and partly the result of our choices unfolding in the present. Our experience of the next moment, the next day, the next decade, is shaped by the choices we make in relationship to where we find ourselves right now. Intended acts of body, speech and mind have consequences; taking these consequences into account offers important guidance in our choices for action.

But these consequences are not fixed or mechanical. Intended actions *tend* toward certain consequences. After all, the interactive field of causality is immense. Sometimes the consequences of our intended actions are submerged in the wide ocean of cause and effect. But, even so, the world tends to respond in a certain way if we act with intentions of greed, hatred or delusion. It tends to respond very differently if we act with motivations of friendliness, generosity, and kindness.

While consequences in the external world may be varied, the inner consequences of our actions are often much clearer, offering us reliable feedback on our choices. For example, we can experience the results of our intentions—karmic consequences— in our bodies. Cumulative habits of greed, hatred or fear affect our muscles one way, while generosity, compassion and reconciliation affect them very differently. Fear can be felt as tightness and tension as the body pulls together in protection. Protecting oneself is an intention, sometimes unnoticed when it becomes chronic. But even unnoticed, the tightness can eventually create physical difficulties.

In meditation, we cease responding to the world habitually. Instead we watch the momentum of the mind: our desires, feelings, thoughts and intentions. Instead of acting on or reacting to them, we give them careful attention. When we don't reinforce them, they quiet down and no longer direct our lives.

The world of suffering and freedom has a lot to do with how we choose to respond to what is given to us, to the present moment itself. What is given may not be to our liking. But, even so, through mindfulness practice we can awaken to the creative potential of choice in how we respond. To choose to respond with aversion, anger, fear, or clinging continues the creation of suffering. To respond with more attention, or without reference to our egoistic attachments, interrupts the cycles of suffering. Creative freedom is not possible if choice is rooted in egoism.

So the world of karma is the world of intention, and the world of intention belongs to the world of right now. Nowhere else. With what intention do you meet this moment? What is your intention for how you do your work, or drive, carry on a conversation, or do someone a favor? If you tend to your intentions with love and care, as you would a garden, your intentions will flower beautifully and bear fruit in your life.

*If beings knew, as I know, the results of giving & sharing,
they would not eat without have given, nor would the stain
of selfishness overcome their minds. Even if it were their last
bite, their last mouthful, they would not eat without having
shared, if there were someone to receive their gift.*
                                              —*Itivuttaka 26*

GENEROSITY

The practice of giving, or *dana* in Pali, has a pre-eminent
place in the teachings of the Buddha. When he taught a gradu-
ated series of practices for people to engage in as they progress
along the path, he always started by talking about the importance
and benefits of the practice of generosity. Based on that foundation he talked about the importance and benefits of the practice
of ethics. Then he discussed the practices of calming the mind,
and after that he described the insight practices, which, supported by a calm and stable mind, lead to enlightenment. Once a person had awakened, the Buddha often instructed him or her to go
out to benefit others, to be of service. Service can be seen as an
act of generosity, so the Buddhist path begins and ends with this
virtue.

Dana refers to the act of giving and to the donation itself.
The Buddha used the word *caga* to refer to the inner virtue of
generosity that ensures that *dana* is connected to the Path. This

use of *caga* is particularly significant because it also means "relinquishment" or "renunciation." An act of generosity entails giving more than is required, customary, or expected relative to one's resources and circumstances. Certainly it involves relinquishment of stinginess, clinging and greed. In addition, generosity entails relinquishing some aspects of one's self-interest, and thus is a giving of one's self. The Buddha stressed that the spiritual efficacy of a gift is dependent not on the amount given but rather on the attitude with which it is given. A small donation that stretches a person of little means is considered of greater spiritual consequence than a large but personally insignificant donation from a wealthy person.

For lay people, the Buddha considered the morally just acquisition of wealth and financial security to be a skillful source of happiness. However, he did not consider wealth to be an end in itself. Its value lay in the uses to which it was put. The Buddha likened a person who enjoyed wealth without sharing it with others to someone digging his own grave. The Buddha also compared the person who righteously earns wealth and gives it to the needy to a person with two eyes. The stingy person was compared to someone with only one eye.

The Buddha understood giving to be a powerful source of merit with long-term benefits both in this life and in lives to come. While the teachings on merit do not carry much meaning for many Western Dharma practitioners, these teachings suggest unseen pathways by which consequences of our actions return to us.

One way that the giver sees his or her generosity return is found in "instant karma," the Buddhist idea that acts that you do have direct consequences on the state of your mind and heart, even as you do them. The consequences of giving are quite wonderful in the present moment; if we are present for them, we can receive these wonderful consequences during the act of giving.

The Buddha emphasized the joy of giving. *Dana* is not meant to be obligatory or done reluctantly. Rather *dana* should be performed when the giver is "delighted before, during, and after giving."

At its most basic level, *dana* in the Buddhist tradition means giving freely without expecting anything in return. The act of giving is purely out of compassion or good will, or the desire for someone else's well-being. Perhaps *dana* is more about how we are than what we do. Through generosity, we cultivate a generous spirit. Generosity of spirit will usually lead to generosity of action, but being a generous person is more important than any particular act of giving; after all, it is possible to give without it being a generous act.

Although giving for the purposes of helping others is an important part of the motivation and joy of giving, the Buddha considered giving for the purpose of attaining *Nibbana* as the highest motivation. For this purpose, "one gives gifts to adorn and beautify the mind." Among these adornments are non-clinging, loving-kindness, and concern for the well being of others.

Some provide from the little they have,
Others who are affluent don't like to give.
An offering given from what little one has
Is worth a thousand times its value.
                                        —*Samyutta Nikaya 1.32*

THE PRACTICE OF GENEROSITY

There are two ways of understanding generosity. One is as a spontaneous and natural expression of an open mind and open heart. When we are connected wholeheartedly with others and the world, it is not a matter of deciding to give; giving simply flows out of us. This type of generosity is, for example, the generosity of a mother with her children. The second way of understanding generosity is as a practice itself, which we can undertake even though it may not automatically be flowing out of us.

As a practice, generosity is not done simply because we think it is a virtuous thing to do. The practice has two important functions. First, it helps connect us with others and with ourselves. Giving creates a relationship between the giver and receiver, so acts of generosity help us to learn more about the nature of our relationships. It also develops those relationships. Practicing generosity together with a meditation practice helps ensure that our spiritual practice doesn't occur aloof from others.

Second, through the practice of generosity we begin to understand where we are closed, where we are holding back, where we feel our fear. We learn what keeps us from being generous. We take on the practice to see where we resist it.

As an intentional practice, there are innumerable exercises in generosity that can be helpful. For example, give yourself a week to give a twenty-dollar bill to someone you don't know. Watch what happens during that week. What does it bring up for you, how do you react, what do you learn about yourself in that situation? Jack Kornfield teaches a practice of acting on every impulse to give, no matter what, during a twenty-four hour period. If that seems too difficult, you could limit it to the practice of giving small things. Another practice is to give a dollar to every homeless person you encounter during a certain period of time.

Generosity is not limited to the giving of material things. We can be generous with our kindness and our receptivity. These forms of generosity are clearly not related to wealth. Generosity can mean the simple giving of a smile or extending ourselves to really listen to a friend. Paradoxically, even being willing to receive the generosity of others can be a form of generosity.

We can also give the gift of fearlessness, a quality that develops as we mature in our practice. As we become increasingly rooted in ethics, wisdom and fearlessness, other beings will have less and less reason to fear us. In a world filled with fear, such fearlessness is a much needed gift. One description of an enlightened person is someone who helps dispel other people's fear.

Buddhist teachings emphasize that the manner in which we give is as important as what we give—we should give with respect, with happiness and joy. When we are practicing generosity, and it does not bring happiness and joy, we should pay close attention to our motivations for giving, and perhaps even re-evaluate whether to give at all.

The freedom of the Buddha is the freedom from all forms of clinging, and the most obvious antidote to clinging is letting go. Because giving certainly involves letting go, it develops our capacity to relinquish clinging. However, the practice of giving entails much more than letting go. It also develops qualities of heart such as generosity, kindness, compassion and warmth. Thus, giving leads us to the heart of Buddhist practice, while helping our practice to be well rounded and heartfelt.

As a merchant carrying great wealth
  In a small caravan avoids a dangerous road:
As someone who loves life
  Avoids poison:
So should you avoid evil deeds.

—*Dhammapada 123*

VIRTUE: THE FIVE PRECEPTS

Buddhist spiritual practice falls into three general categories known in Pali as *sila*, *samadhi* and *pañña*, which can be translated into English as virtue, meditation and wisdom, respectively. They function like three legs of a tripod; it is essential to cultivate all three. Wisdom and meditation will not develop without virtue. Developing virtue and understanding the full depths of its possibilities requires wisdom and meditation.

No single English word adequately translates *sila*. Sometimes, in its etymological origins, *sila* is said to come from the word for "bed". Certainly we can see it as the bedrock or foundation upon which the rest of our spiritual practice is built. Sooner or later, anyone who begins to develop some sensitivity through mindfulness practice will discover that without the foundation of virtue, the depths of sensitivity are hard to develop.

Sila is usually translated as "virtue" or "ethics," but we need to be careful not to confuse it with Western ideas of virtue and ethics. A traditional foundation of Western ethics is commandments and values often handed down from a god. These values include ideas about right and wrong, good and evil, and absolute rules that we have to live by. This approach to ethics leads easily to guilt, an emotion that is pervasive in the West, but which is considered unnecessary and counterproductive in Buddhism.

Buddhism understands virtue and ethics pragmatically, based not on ideas of good and bad, but rather on the observation that some actions lead to suffering and some actions lead to happiness and freedom. A Buddhist asks, "Does this action lead to increased suffering or increased happiness, for myself and others?" This pragmatic approach is more conducive to investigation than to guilt.

As guidelines for virtue and ethical behavior, the Buddha formulated precepts for us to follow. For lay people, there are five basic guidelines. These are 1) to abstain from killing, 2) to abstain from stealing, 3) to abstain from sexual misconduct, 4) to abstain from lying, and 5) to abstain from intoxicants such as drugs or alcohol.

The Buddha referred to these five in different ways, giving us different perspectives from which to understand them. Sometimes he called them the "five training rules" (*pancasikkha*), sometimes "five virtues" (*pancasila*), and sometimes simply as "the five things" or the "five truths" (*pancadhamma*). The expression "the five things" might seem odd, but perhaps it helps to free us from fixed ideas about what these "things" are, and how they function.

There are three ways of understanding these "five things." The first is as rules of behavior. These are not considered commandments; rather the Buddha called them "training rules." We voluntarily take on the training precepts as a discipline for the support of our spiritual training. Following them promotes the development of meditation, wisdom and compassion.

As training rules, the precepts are understood as rules of restraint. They are phrased as "For the sake of my training, I vow not to kill, not to steal," and so forth. We agree to hold back on certain impulses. Instead of following our inclination to kill a mosquito or steal pencils from work, we hold back and try to bring mindfulness to the discomfort we are impulsively reacting to. Rather than focusing on whether the actions are bad or immoral, we use these restraints as mirrors to study ourselves, to understand our reactions and motivations, and to reflect on the consequences of our actions.

Following the training rules offers us a powerful form of protection. Primarily, the precepts protect us from ourselves, from the suffering we cause others and ourselves when we act unskillfully.

The second way the Buddha talked about the precepts was as principles of virtue. The fundamental principles that underlie all five precepts are compassion, not causing harm, and generosity. We follow the precepts out of compassion, out of a sense of the suffering of others, and out of the possibility that others can be free of suffering. We also live by the precepts out of compassion for ourselves. We want to be careful about our intentional actions, how we act, how we speak, even the kinds of thoughts we pursue.

So that the precepts do not become a rigid ideal that we live by, we practice them together with the principle of non-harming. We can keep in check any tendency to create harm through narrow minded or callous use of the precepts by asking ourselves, "Is this action causing harm to myself or others?" The understanding of what causes harm brings humanity to the precepts.

Living by the precepts is itself an act of generosity; we give a wonderful gift of protection to ourselves and to others. Indeed, one pragmatic reason to follow the precepts as rules of restraint is to bring joy to our lives. Many people meditate because they feel they are lacking joy and happiness. According to the Buddha, one of the best ways to cultivate and appreciate joy is to live a virtuous life.

The third way the Buddha talked about the precepts was as qualities of a person's character. The Buddha described someone who was spiritually well developed as endowed with the five virtues. The Buddha said that once you reach a certain level of awakening, it is simply not possible to break the precepts. Following the precepts is a direct by-product of having discovered freedom.

In summary, these five things can be understood as rules of training, as principles to guide our actions, and as a description of how an awakened person acts. The world needs more people with the intention, sensitivity and purity of heart represented by the five precepts.

May the precepts be a source of joy for everyone.

Better than one hundred years lived
Devoid of insight and unsettled,
Is one day lived
With insight and absorbed in meditation.
—Dhammapada 111

BRIEF INSTRUCTIONS FOR SITTING MEDITATION

Take a comfortable and alert posture, either on the floor or on a chair. Gently close your eyes and establish a sense of presence within your body. It is often helpful to start a period of meditation with two or three deep breaths to establish a clear connection with the body and the breath, and to shed some of the surface preoccupations of the mind. Then, direct your attention to simply but consciously noticing the physical sensations of breathing in and breathing out without trying to control or manipulate your breath.

As you become familiar with your breathing, rest your attention in the area of your body where the breath is clearest or easiest to attend to. This can be the rising and falling of the abdomen, the movement of the chest, or the sensation of air passing through the nostrils. To help maintain the connection between the physical sensations of breathing and awareness, people often find it useful to gently, silently label the inhalations and exhalations as "rising" and "falling" or "in" and "out."

Because mindfulness of breathing develops our capacity to be settled and aware in the present, we give some priority to maintaining an attentive focus on the breath during sitting meditation. Whenever you become lost in preoccupation with the surface chatter of the mind, gently, without judgment, reestablish your attention on the breath.

However, when some other sensation or experience becomes so strong that you find it difficult to remain attentive to the breath, let go of the breath and allow the stronger sensation to be the center of attention. You may find it useful to distinguish between the foreground and background of awareness. Initially, place your breathing in the foreground of awareness, allowing all other sensations and experiences to remain in the background. As long as you can maintain the breath in the foreground without straining, let the background experiences simply be. When some physical, emotional, or mental experience displaces the breath in the foreground, take this as the new resting place for your awareness.

As an aid to remaining mindfully focused on an experience that has come to the foreground, you may find it useful to gently and softly name it with a mental note. Sounds can be labeled as "hearing, hearing," burning sensations as "burning, burning," joy as "joy, joy," and so on. What is important is to sense, feel, and remain present as fully as possible for whatever experience is being noted. Maintain an open awareness of it for however long it remains in the foreground of attention, noticing how, if at all, the experience changes. Once an experience is no longer predominant, or it is sufficiently acknowledged to no longer demand your attention, return your attention to the breathing.

Another way to describe mindfulness practice is to say that you consciously and clearly rest your attention on the breath until something strongly distracts you from it. When this occurs, the so-called "distraction" becomes the focus of the meditation. Actually, mindfulness practice has no distractions, only something new to pay attention to. Nothing is outside the scope of mindfulness meditation. The full range of our humanity is allowed to unfold within the light of our mindfulness. Physical sensations, feelings, emotions, thoughts, mental states, moods, and intentions are all included.

Throughout your meditation, keep the attention soft and relaxed, while alert and precise. If you can distinguish between the ideas, concepts, images, and stories associated with some experience on the one hand, and the immediate and direct felt-sense of the experience on the other, let mindfulness rest with the direct experience. Notice the physical or mental sensations that are actually, tangibly arising in the present. Notice what happens to them as you are mindful of them. Do they get stronger, weaker, or stay the same?

Notice also your relationship to your experience. Do you notice aversion, desire, appreciation, judgment, condemnation, fear, grasping, pride, or any other reaction? The realization, for example, that a painful physical sensation is different from your reaction to it can help you find balance in the midst of discomfort. It is also important to be mindful of when your reaction to an experience is more pronounced than the experience itself. When it is, your reaction can become the resting place of awareness. Do not participate in your thoughts or stories but simply and silently be aware of what is actually occurring in the body and in the mind.

As we learn to be alertly and calmly present in our meditation, a deeper intimacy with ourselves and with the world will arise. As we cultivate our ability to remain mindful without interfering, judging, avoiding, or clinging to our direct experience, wellsprings of insight and wisdom have a chance to surface.

When mindfulness of breathing is developed and cultivated, it is of great fruit and great benefit. When mindfulness of breathing is developed and cultivated, it fulfills the four foundations of mindfulness. When the four foundations of mindfulness are developed and cultivated, they fulfill the seven enlightenment factors. When the seven enlightenment factors are developed and cultivated, they fulfill true knowledge and deliverance.

—Majjhima Nikaya 118.15

MINDFULNESS OF BREATHING

Mindfulness meditation usually begins with awareness of breathing. In fact, breath is the foundation of many forms of Buddhist meditation practice. My Zen teacher in Japan said that mindfulness of breathing is enough, in and of itself, for a person to become fully awakened.

The repertoire of religious practices of the world contains a wealth of useful breath meditations. Many involve patterns of conscious breathing: breathing long and deeply; emphasizing the exhalation over the inhalation; breathing fast or slow, through the nose or mouth; intentionally pausing between breaths; directing the breath to different parts of the body. In mindfulness practice we are not trying to change the breath. We are simply attending to the breath as it is, getting to know it as it is, regardless of how it is: shallow or deep, long or short, slow or fast, smooth or rough, coarse or refined, constricted or loose. For the practice of mindfulness there is no ideal breath. If we impose a rigid pattern on our breathing, we might miss how our own particular physical, emotional, and spiritual patterns are expressed through breathing.

Because of the mind's tendency to be scattered and easily distracted by daydreams and thoughts, we use the breath to help anchor us to the present. By repeatedly coming back to rest in the breath, we are countering the strong forces of distraction. This trains the mind, heart, and body to become settled and unified on one thing, at one place, at one time. If you are sitting in meditation and your mind is on what you did at work today, your mind and body are not in the same place at the same time. When we are fragmented in this way we easily lose touch with a holistic sense of ourselves.

Mindfulness of breathing can be a powerful ally in our lives. With steady awareness of our inhalations and exhalations, the breath can become an equanimous constant through the ups and downs of our daily life. By resting with and perhaps even enjoying the cycles of breathing, we are less likely to be caught up in the emotional and mental events that pass through us. Repeatedly returning to the breath can be a highly effective training in letting go of patterns of identification and holding that freeze the mind and heart.

Since our breath is not independent from our mental and emotional life, often our emotions, attitudes, and concerns are expressed in the way we breathe. Patterns of breathing change with our varied emotions. With fear and sadness the breath can be constricted. With anger it can be strong and forced. With peace and calm it can be easy and relaxed. The etymological root of the word anxious is 'choking,' and choking or constricting the breath is how we sometimes control or hold back excitement or energetic states of being. Remember that in mindfulness practice we simply notice what is happening without adding our judgments about how our breath, our inner life or we should be.

However, attention, just like other mental states, can affect the breath in its own way, often by slowing and calming it, but sometimes by releasing it from our holding. Remembering to be aware of the breath can lubricate difficult situations. This is because the power of attention itself is helpful in any situation, and also because attention directed to the breath can keep our breath and us from becoming rigid.

Mindfulness of the body, when developed and cultivated, is of great fruit and great benefit.

—Majjhima Nikaya 119.2

THE BODY AT THE CENTER: MINDFULNESS OF THE BODY IN THE PRACTICE-INSTRUCTIONS OF THE BUDDHA

I did not begin my Buddhist practice with any intention to discover my body. I had no idea that the body had any importance to the path of practice, except as something to place on the meditation cushion. Even during the early months and years of my meditation practice when my body painfully revealed areas of tightness, tension, and psychological holding patterns, I was convinced that these physical difficulties were nuisances to be ignored or transcended rather than the actual substance and unfolding of practice. Slowly, over the years as my body began to come alive, I was, and still am, repeatedly surprised at how much awareness, love and compassion are found in and through the body. I have learned that mindfulness of the body is the foundation of mindfulness practice, and one of the best friends we have for integrating that practice into daily life.

The Buddha himself said, "There is one thing that when cultivated and regularly practiced leads to deep spiritual intention, to peace, to mindfulness and clear comprehension, to vision and knowledge, to a happy life here and now, and to the culmination of wisdom and awakening. And what is that one thing? Mindfulness centered on the body." Elsewhere, the Buddha said, "If the body is not cultivated, the mind cannot be cultivated. If the body is cultivated then the mind can be cultivated."

You can find shelf after shelf of Western books on Buddhism that make virtually no mention of the body, thus giving or reinforcing the impression that Buddhism is an intellectual or mentally oriented religion. In contrast to this impression, I understand Buddhist practice, especially the practice of mindfulness, to be an invitation to experience our bodies and to embody our experience. Or as the Scripture on the Four Foundations of Mindfulness puts it, "to experience the breath **in** the breath and the body **in** the body." Distancing himself from metaphysics and speculations, the Buddha was interested in understanding how we experience and perceive directly through our psycho-physical senses. He taught that for the purpose of awakening and spiritual freedom, everything we need to realize of the world is found within our body. Without rejecting the notion of an objective world, the Buddha focused so much on the role of the senses and perception that he repeatedly claimed that "within this very fathom-long body, with its perceptions and inner sense, lies the world, the cause of the world, the cessation of the world, and the path that leads to the cessation of the world."

During my early *Vipassana* practice in Thailand, Achaan Buddhadasa said at the opening of a ten-day retreat, "Do not do anything that takes you out of your body." I carried this—for me puzzling—instruction with me during the ten-day retreat, and I began to realize how often my center of attention and gravity

48

were projected in front of me as I so frequently reached forward to grasp or identify with something outside of myself. The anticipation of lunch or the end of a meditation period, the rehashing of memories, the planning for future events, and the desire for or aversion to emotions or states of mind all contributed to a sense of not being physically centered on myself. Often I would feel as if I was ahead of myself either by actually leaning forward, or more usually and more subtly by feeling my "center of gravity" projected forward. In the course of the ten-day retreat, I began to learn to settle back into my own center of gravity and to align my body in a balanced vertical posture. The more settled I felt in my body, the more sensitive I became to ever subtler movements away from center caused by ever subtler attachments and aversions of the mind. Gradually I learned that mindfulness of the body is one of the best windows I have into an honest view of my inner life.

In contrast to a trend in western culture to posit a radical duality between the body and the mind, the Buddha saw the human mind and body as intimately interconnected. When we repress or suppress aspects of our emotional and cognitive life we tend to disconnect ourselves from our body. The exploration and awakening of the body from the inside through mindfulness and awareness can result in a rediscovery of suppressed emotions, and also a greater capacity to feel emotions, to be *sentient* beings.

Mindfulness of the body can greatly facilitate our capacity for being present for painful or overwhelming emotions by helping us recognize that the body is the container for those emotions. Buddhist psychology teaches that emotions are virtually always embodied and so can be felt in the body. Sometimes fear involves a tightening of the stomach, anger a heated face, joy a tingling or warmth in the chest, and restlessness an energy coursing through the arms. By focusing on the bodily sensations produced by difficult emotions, we can more easily remain present for them and allow mindfulness to reveal their deeper nature.

Our western culture has devoted a tremendous amount of resources to strengthening our predilection to treat the body as an object to be manipulated. "Body consciousness" has come to refer to the external image that we not only project but also create with the help of cosmetics, hair stylists, the fashion and advertising industries, and the local gym. By contrast, in mindfulness practice we are developing a form of body consciousness that involves a subjective awareness of the body from the inside. This inner subjective world is the source of our vitality. Objectifying the body can disconnect us from that sense of aliveness.

When we begin to be aware of how we actually and directly experience the body from the inside, we begin to learn that the body is an awareness and a process and not simply a "thing." The Buddhist tradition distinguishes a variety of "bodies"— the energy body, the bliss body, the transformation body, the diamond body, the karmic body, and the awareness body. A meditator can experience all of these different bodies, often as a flow of energy or field of attention.

In developing mindfulness of the body, *Vipassana* students are counteracting not only the cultural forces that reinforce a solid and objective body image but also our own psychological forces that do so. Our psycho-physical holding patterns such as the tightening of the stomach, shoulders or jaws help create a sense of false or illusionary solidity as we shield ourselves from whatever is fearful or painful. As mindfulness practice develops we learn to trust our inner experience, our awareness, and our capacity for being present for even difficult states of being.

However, mindfulness practice does not lead to rejection of all body images and self imaging. Rather, we learn the flexibility to move easily between appropriate body images and the openness and imageless-ness of direct experience. There are times when a strong self image is crucial, and other times when it is a great limitation. And regardless of the value of open, egoless states, we must remember that holding on to such states can cause great suffering. Mindfulness practice is less about attaining some particular state than about attaining freedom and flexibility within all states.

As meditation opens the ego boundaries that the world may or may not require of us, mindfulness of the body helps to create a healthy center within the openness. Maintaining an openness to the world is safer if one remains aware of what is happening within the body. The body can provide, more readily than any other avenue, a tremendous amount of information about how we are affected by and reacting to any given situation. Without this information there is the danger that contracted or expansive states of being will blind us to many aspects of who we are—that we will lose our sense of presence to either external situations or people or to an inner world of thoughts and feelings.

Within the Theravada Buddhist tradition there are a number of different styles of mindfulness practice. Some focus almost exclusively on mindfulness of the body. Others include, to various degrees, the other aspects of our humanity—feelings, emotions, thoughts, mental states and mental experiences. However even among these latter styles, mindfulness of the body remains, throughout one's practice, the most foundational of the foundations of mindfulness practice. In the Scripture on the Four

Foundations of Mindfulness, under the foundation of the body, the Buddha included attention to the breath, body sensations of all types, physical posture, the body in activity, and the systematic exploration of the entire body. I believe that the other three foundations of mindfulness are best understood after one has begun to stabilize or awaken one's awareness in the body.

Various streams of the Mahayana Buddhist tradition have similarly placed great stress on the importance of the body. Several Mahayana scriptures enthusiastically insist that "the body itself is *bodhi* (awakening)." One tantric song says, "Here in this body are the sacred rivers: here are the sun and moon, as well as all the pilgrimage places. I have not encountered another temple as blissful as my own body." The Japanese Zen tradition has also stressed the importance of the conscious participation of the body in practice. The Zen master Dogen, teaching that Zen practice involves the unification of the body and mind, wrote that "mindfulness of the body is the body's mindfulness."

In the end, the central position that the body has in the Buddhist tradition does not mean that we need to direct our attention willfully toward the body as if awareness and the body were two separate things. Rather the teaching of mindfulness of the body is an invitation for us to wake up to the awareness that is already present in the body. Practice is not directing or creating something. The beginning and end of practice is the awakening of what is already there—within our bodies, hearts and minds.

There's no fire like that of lust,
No grasping like that of hate,
No snare like that of delusion,
No river like that of craving.

—*Dhammapada 251*

MINDFULNESS OF EMOTIONS

Bringing awareness to our emotions helps us to have straightforward or uncomplicated emotions. No emotion is inappropriate within the field of our mindfulness practice. We are trying to allow them to exist as they arise, without reactivity, without the additional complications of judgment, evaluation, preferences, aversion, desires, clinging or resistance.

The Buddha once asked a student, "If a person is struck by an arrow is it painful?" The student replied, "It is." The Buddha then asked, "If the person is struck by a second arrow, is that even more painful? The student replied again, "It is." The Buddha then explained, "In life, we cannot always control the first arrow. However, the second arrow is our reaction to the first. This second arrow is optional."

As long as we are alive we can expect painful experiences—the first arrow. To condemn, judge, criticize, hate, or deny the first arrow is like being struck by a second arrow. Many times the first arrow is out of our control but the arrow of reactivity is not.

Often the significant suffering associated with an emotion is not the emotion itself but the way we relate to it. Do we feel it to be unacceptable? Justified? Do we hate it? Feel pride in it? Are we ashamed of it? Do we tense around it? Are we afraid of how we are feeling?

Mindfulness itself does not condemn our reactions. Rather it is honestly aware of what happens to us and how we react to it. The more cognizant and familiar we are with our reactivity the more easily we can feel, for example, uncomplicated grief or straightforward joy, not mixed up with guilt, anger, remorse, embarrassment, judgment or other reactions. Freedom in Buddhism is not freedom from emotions; it is freedom from complicating them.

There are four aspects to mindfulness of emotions: recognition, naming, acceptance and investigation. There is no need to practice with all four each time an emotion is present. You can experiment to find out how they each encourage a non-reactive awareness towards emotions.

Recognition: A basic principle of mindfulness is that we cannot experience freedom and spaciousness unless we recognize what is happening. Recognizing certain emotions as they arise can sometimes be difficult. We have been taught that some emotions are inappropriate, or we are afraid of them, or simply don't like them. For example, when I first started practice, I became angry when my practice on retreat didn't go the way I expected it to. But I had an image of myself as someone who was not angry, so I didn't acknowledge the anger. Not until I recognized the anger could the retreat really begin for me. The more we learn to recognize the range of our emotions, including the subtlest ones, the more familiar and comfortable we become with them. As this happens, their grip on us relaxes.

Naming: A steady and relaxed mental noting, or naming of the emotion of the moment—"joy", "anger", "frustration", "happiness", "boredom", "contentment", "desire" and the like—encourages us to stay present with what is central in our experience. Naming is a powerful way to keep us from identifying with strong emotions. There are many ways that we are caught by emotions: we can feel justified in them, condemn them, feel ashamed of them, or enthralled with them. Naming helps us step outside of the identification to a more neutral point of observation: "It's like this." Folk tales tell of the dragon losing its power when it is named. Likewise, emotions can lose their power over us when they are named.

Acceptance: In mindfulness, we simply allow emotions to be present, whatever they may be. This does not mean condoning or justifying our feelings. Formal meditation practice offers us the extraordinary opportunity to practice unconditional acceptance of our emotions. This does not mean expressing emotion, but letting emotions move through us without inhibitions, resistance, or encouragement. To facilitate acceptance, we can try to see that the emotion has arisen because certain conditions have come together. For example, if you had a flat tire on the way to work, and your boss gave you a new assignment with a tight deadline after you finally arrived, you might feel frustrated or angry. If your boss gave you that same assignment on a morning after you'd had a good night's sleep and heard some great news about your stock options, you might feel excited or challenged. If we can see emotions as arising from a particular set of conditions, we can more easily accept them, and not take them personally.

Investigation: This entails dropping any fixed ideas we have about an emotion and looking at it afresh. Emotions are composite events, made up of bodily sensations, thoughts, feelings, motivations and attitudes. Investigation is not abstract analysis. Instead it is more of a sensory awareness exercise: we feel our way into the present moment experience of the emotions. Particularly useful is the practice of investigating the bodily sensations of an emotion. The correlation between emotions and their physical manifestation is so strong that when we resist or suppress our emotions, we often do the same with sensations in parts of our bodies. Waking up to our body through mindfulness practice also allows us to wake up to our capacity to feel emotions. If we let the body be the container for the emotion, we can more easily disengage from the thoughts around the emotion—the stories, analysis, or attempts to fix the situation—and simply rest with the present moment experience.

Mindfulness of emotions helps us to come to a place where we don't react habitually to our inner urges and emotions. That place is a good foundation from which to look carefully at situations and make wise decisions. The point of Buddhist meditation is not to become emotionally neutral. Through it, we can open up to our full capacity to feel emotions and be sensitive to the world around us, and yet not be overwhelmed by what we feel.

The mind, hard to control,
Flighty—alighting where it wishes
One does well to tame.
The disciplined mind brings happiness.
The mind, hard to see,
Subtle—alighting where it wishes
The sage protects.
The watched mind brings happiness.
Dhammapada 35–36

MINDFULNESS OF THOUGHTS

Sometimes people think the point of meditation is to stop thinking—to have a silent mind. This does happen occasionally, but it is not necessarily the point of meditation. Thoughts are an important part of life, and mindfulness practice is not supposed to be a struggle against them. We can benefit more by being friends with our thoughts than by regarding them as unfortunate distractions. In mindfulness, we are not stopping thoughts as much as overcoming any preoccupation we have with them.

However, mindfulness is not thinking about things, either. It is a non-discursive observation of our life in all its aspects. In those moments when thinking predominates, mindfulness is the clear and silent awareness that we are thinking. A piece of advice I found helpful and relaxing was when someone said, "For the purpose of meditation, nothing is particularly worth thinking about." Thoughts can come and go as they wish, and the meditator does not need to become involved with them. We are not interested in engaging in the content of our thoughts. Mindfulness of thinking is simply recognizing that we are thinking.

In meditation, when thoughts are subtle and in the background, or when random thoughts pull us away from awareness of the present, all we have to do is resume mindfulness of breathing. However, when our preoccupation with thoughts is stronger than our ability to let go of them easily, then we direct mindfulness to being clearly aware that thinking is occurring.

Strong bouts of thinking are fuelled largely by identification and preoccupation with thoughts. By clearly observing our thinking, we step outside the field of identification. Thinking will usually then soften to a calm and unobtrusive stream.

Sometimes thinking can be strong and compulsive even while we are aware of it. When this happens, one approach is to notice how such thinking affects the body, physically and energetically. It may cause pressure in the head, tension in the forehead, tightness of the shoulders, or a buzzing as if the head were filled with thousands of bumblebees. Let your mindfulness feel the sensations of tightness, pressure, or whatever you discover. To be caught up in the story of these preoccupying thoughts is easy, but if you feel the physical sensation of thinking, then you are bringing attention to the present moment rather than the story line of the thoughts.

When a particular theme keeps reappearing in your thinking, most likely it is triggered by a strong emotion. In that case, no matter how many times you recognize a repeated thought-concern and come back to the breath, the concern is liable to keep reappearing if the associated emotion isn't recognized. For example, people who plan a lot often find that planning thoughts arise out of apprehension. If the fear is not acknowledged, it will become a factory of new planning thoughts. So, if there is a repetitive thought pattern, see if you can discover an emotion associated with it, and then practice mindfulness of the emotion. Ground yourself in the present moment in the emotion itself. When you acknowledge the emotion, often the thoughts it engenders will cease.

Thoughts are a huge part of our lives. Many of us spend much time inhabiting the cognitive world of stories and ideas. Mindfulness practice won't stop the thinking, but it will help prevent us from compulsively following thoughts that have appeared. And this in turn will help us become more balanced, so that our physical, emotional and cognitive sides all work together as a whole.

Beings are
    owners of their karma,
    heirs of their karma,
    born of their karma,
    related to their karma,
    supported by their karma.
Whatever karma they do, for good or for ill,
    Of that they are the heirs.

                                 —Anguttara Nikaya V.57

MINDFULNESS OF INTENTIONS

Buddhism offers us a challenge: is it possible to live a life with no suffering? One of the most direct ways to bring ease and happiness into our mindfulness practice and into our lives is by investigating our intentions. While our activities have consequences in both the external world and the internal world, the happiness and freedom to which the Buddha pointed belong to the inner world of our intentions and dispositions. This is one of the prime reasons why the Buddha placed such emphasis on attending to our intentions.

Buddhist practice encourages a deep appreciation of the present moment, which strengthens our ability to respond creatively in the present rather than acting according to our habits and dispositions. Mindfulness places us where choice is possible. The greater our awareness of our intentions, the greater our freedom to choose. People who do not see their choices do not believe they have choices. They tend to respond automatically, blindly influenced by their circumstances and conditioning. Mindfulness, by helping us notice our impulses before we act, gives us the opportunity to decide whether to act and how to act.

According to traditional Buddhist teaching, every mind-moment involves an intention. This suggests the phenomenal subtlety with which choices operate in our lives. Few of us keep our bodies still, except perhaps in meditation or in sleep. Each of the constant movements in our arms, hands and legs is preceded by a volitional impulse, usually unnoticed. Intentions are present even in such seemingly minute and usually unnoticed decisions as where to direct our attention or which thoughts to pursue. Just as drops of water will eventually fill a bathtub, so the accumulation of these small choices shapes who we are.

Our intentions—noticed or unnoticed, gross or subtle—contribute either to our suffering or to our happiness. Intentions are sometimes called seeds. The garden you grow depends on the seeds you plant and water. Long after a deed is done, the trace or momentum of the intention behind it remains as a seed, conditioning our future happiness or unhappiness. If we water intentions of greed or hate, their inherent suffering will sprout, both while we act on them and in the future in the form of reinforced habits, tensions and painful memories. If we nourish intentions of love or generosity, the inherent happiness and openness of those states will become a more frequent part of our life.

Some volitional acts actually hamper the awakening of awareness. One example of this is intentional lying. The fear of discovery, the continued need for deceit that often follows, and the avoidance of the truth tend to reinforce the mind's tendency to preoccupation, which is the opposite of wakefulness.

An important function of mindfulness practice is to help us understand the immediate and longer-term consequences of our intended actions. This understanding helps ensure that our choices are wiser than those based only on our likes and preferences. Having a realistic and informed sense of consequences keeps our "good" intentions from being naive intentions. It can also guide us in knowing which choices support our spiritual practice and which detract from it.

We can bring awareness of intention into mindfulness practice in a number of ways.

Perhaps the most significant is to reflect carefully on your deepest intention. What is your heart's deepest wish? What is of greatest value or priority for you? Mindfulness practice connected to your deepest intention will bear a different result than practice connected to more superficial concerns. The business-person who undertakes mindfulness practice as a means of stress reduction in order to gain an edge over the competition will sow the seeds for very different results than the one who undertakes mindfulness to strengthen his or her compassionate service to others. When the effort to be mindful is fueled by greed, that very effort also fortifies the tension and insensitivity of greed. When the effort is fueled by loving-kindness, it energizes the inner openness and sensitivity of loving-kindness.

I believe that a daily sitting practice is extremely beneficial. But I believe there is even more benefit in spending a few minutes each day reflecting on our deepest intentions. In a busy life, we can easily forget our fundamental values and motivations. To remind ourselves of them allows our choices to be informed by them. Furthermore, when we drop below the surface cravings and aversions of the mind to discover our deeper stirrings, we tap a tremendous power of inspiration and motivation. For example, at one point, I took on the practice of consciously reflecting on my intention for each task of the day, allowing my deeper sense of intention to inform each one. Even the seemingly mundane activity of going to the grocery store became an opportunity to strengthen my intention to connect with people with care and compassion. This simple practice brought me a great deal of joy.

Another way of including intention in our practice is to pause briefly before initiating any new activity, which allows us to discern our motivation. Being aware of an intention after an action is started is useful but it can be like trying to stop a ball after you have thrown it. The momentum has been set in motion.

We can investigate the intentions behind major activities and decisions such as work, relationships, or what we do during our free time. What is the motivation and how does it relate to our deepest intentions? Similarly we can investigate the intentions that shape our decisions around such minor matters as what and when to eat, how we drive, what we read or watch on television. Is the choice based on fear, aversion, loneliness, or addiction, or on generosity or caring for ourselves wisely? Different motivations are not necessarily good or bad. They may, however, create very different consequences even when the external actions that they generate look the same.

Trying to bring attention to all our motivations may be overwhelming. It can be useful to choose one activity at a time to look at more carefully. For example, spend a week becoming a connoisseur of your many intentions around eating, shopping, or cleaning house.

Perhaps one of the more significant applications of mindfulness of intention concerns speech. We often speak without reflection. Attention to the multiple reasons underlying what we say is one of the most powerful windows into our hearts. Speech is seldom a simple offering of information or expression of caring. It is closely tied to how we see ourselves, how we want others to see us, and our hopes and fears. Distinguishing wholesome intentions from unwholesome intentions can serve as a useful criterion for when to speak and when to take refuge in wise silence. Speech can powerfully support or undermine a spiritual practice.

Attention and intention are two cornerstones of Buddhist practice. Bringing attention to intention does not, as some fear, lead to a life of endless effort at monitoring ourselves. Self-consciousness and self-preoccupation may be exhausting, but not awareness. As we become clearer and wiser about our intentions, we find greater ease. We begin to act with less and less self-centered concern.

To follow the Buddhist path of mindfulness to its end—to the cessation of suffering, to the Deathless—takes great dedication. The wiser we are about our intentions in practice, the greater the usefulness of that effort.

May you wisely notice your intentions and may doing so help to alleviate suffering everywhere.

As a bee gathers nectar
And moves on without harming
The flower, its color, or its fragrance,
Just so should a sage move through a village.
                                    —*Dhammapada 49*

BEING A NATURALIST

In mindfulness meditation we learn to be present for things as they are. In doing so, it can be useful to assume the attitude of a naturalist. A naturalist simply observes nature without interfering or imposing his or her views. If a wolf eats a deer, a naturalist watches without judgment. If a plant produces a stunningly beautiful blossom, a naturalist leaves it alone, not succumbing to the desire to take it home.

In meditation, we observe ourselves much as a naturalist observes nature: without repressing, denying, grasping or defending anything. This means that we observe our life with a non-interfering presence. We can see our anger, depression, fear, happiness, joy, pain and pleasure directly, as they are, without complications. The naturalist's perspective is one of respect for what is observed. The word "re-spect" is a nice synonym for mindfulness practice because it literally means to "look again."

Often we complicate our observation of ourselves by taking

things personally. Of course we can't deny that our sorrows and joys, challenges and blessings, emotions and thoughts are happening to us. But when we take them personally we let ourselves be defined by them: the presence of anger means I am an angry person. A generous act taken personally is proof that I am a generous person. While the common tendency of taking things personally may seem innocent, it often unnecessarily complicates our relationship with what is happening. We can easily become muddled in confusions regarding such issues as personal identity, image, and expectation.

From the naturalist perspective, one does not see "my anger" or "my generosity." Rather, they are simply observed as "the anger" or "the impulse of generosity." Such a switch of perspective can be particularly helpful with physical pain. When taken personally, "my pain" can easily lead to burdensome feelings of responsibility and entanglement. When we see it as "the pain," it tends to be easier for us to remain disentangled and lighter.

Another way we complicate our lives is by assigning values of good and bad to our experiences. For a naturalist there is no good or bad; the natural world just unfolds. During mindfulness meditation we do not need to judge our experience as either good or bad. We simply watch how things are and how they unfold.

By cultivating a naturalist's perspective during meditation, it is possible to develop a capacity to be non-reactive. From this non-reactive perspective, we can more easily explore how to respond wisely to whatever circumstances we find ourselves in. Once we have seen clearly, there may well be a need for action or involvement. For example, a naturalist may decide to remove a non-native plant from a delicate eco-system. Likewise, through non-reactively witnessing our anger or greed, we may decide to uproot them.

Because of our wonderful powers of observation and reflection, human beings can be both observer and observed. We can be both the naturalist and the nature. We are nature seeing itself. Through our capacity to see clearly, we can be nature freeing itself.

Who once was inattentive
   But now is not,
Illumines the world
   Like the moon set free from a cloud.
                              —*Dhammapada 172*

ACCORDING WITH NATURE

All spiritual practice involves change, or a wish for change: to go from a state of suffering to a state without suffering, to go from agitation to calm, to go from a closed heart to an open, compassionate heart. When people first come to a spiritual practice the desire—even the need—for change is often quite clear. Conversely, in some advanced Buddhist practices the desire for change may be so subtle that it may go unnoticed. For example, one may learn the practice of simply accepting things as they are, without wanting change. But even here there is change—from a state of non-acceptance to a state of acceptance.

It is important for us to reflect on our relationship to the process of seeking change. Are there healthy and unhealthy ways of bringing about change? One way to think of this is to look at the distinction between change that accords with nature and change as an act of ego.

Consider how a skillful gardener supports the growth of a

flower. The gardener doesn't tug on a seed sprout to help the plant grow or pull open the petals to open a blossom. Rather he or she nourishes and protects the plant, and so lets it grow and flower in line with its nature.

In the same way, much of what sustains our life occurs without our needing to intervene. For example, the body knows how to take care of itself in a way that the mind could never possibly understand. The conscious mind cannot control everything related to the pumping of the heart, the circulation of blood, and the workings of the immune system. What our bodies do without our conscious awareness is simply astounding! Our main role in these processes is to nourish and protect.

In contrast to this natural unfolding, there is change imposed by the ego, out of our insecurity, fear, hostility, greed, or ambition. And because of our phenomenal ability for abstract thinking, we easily impose our world of ideas on top of nature rather than patiently allowing nature to show us what is needed and how we can come into accord with it. One concept we often impose on our experience is an assumption of permanence, which can put us at odds with the inherent impermanence of all natural processes. Another concept that can inhibit the expression of our nature is a fixed image of ourselves, which can easily propel us to conform to "shoulds" and "shouldn'ts."

I believe that spiritual practice unfolds most smoothly when we find how to accord ourselves with nature. A useful metaphor for this is a river. To enter the spiritual life fully is to enter a stream that eventually carries you to the great ocean. All you have to do is to get into the river and stay in it. Trust, persistence, mindfulness, clarity and insight help us float in the river. Once we are floating, the nature of a river is to carry us effortlessly to the ocean. If we fight the river, if we fight against the current, we can exhaust ourselves trying to go against the natural flow.

The river metaphor is quite different from the popular metaphor that likens the spiritual path to climbing a mountain—which suggests hard, constant, and willful uphill effort, and can lend itself to an ego-driven spirituality. The trek is hard, suggesting that not everyone can make it. The mountain peak may be quite narrow, suggesting it can only hold a few people at a time. In contrast, the ocean is big enough to hold everyone.

The river metaphor is expressive of a practice of according with nature, with truth. This does not mean that spiritual practice requires nothing of us. A fast river may require our attention and navigation to stay in the current, off the rocks, and out of the eddies. Practice requires mindfulness and investigation, supported by calmness and inner stability, to discover nature and how to accord ourselves with it. Often this entails learning how to leave ourselves alone, how not to interfere with the natural unfolding and healing that will occur if we give them a chance. Our conscious mind may not know what is supposed to unfold. Like a flower that needs water and fertilizer, our inner life opens in its varied ways when it is ready, if we nourish it with attentiveness, compassion and acceptance.

To work with nature we need to study it thoroughly. One way to do this is to investigate all the ways we work against nature by being judgmental, hostile, demanding, hurried, unkind or ungenerous.

Another important way to study nature is through mindfulness of the body. Our bodies are, after all, a clear expression of nature. The body is perhaps our most intimate connection to nature. To be mindful of the body is to be interested in what wants to move within the body, what wants expression. Many of our volitions, desires, fears, aspirations, understandings and emotions reside in the body. To resist nature is to keep these frozen within the body. But the opposite, to act on them blindly, also goes against nature.

To accord with nature is to discover that you *are* nature. In Buddhism, there is the saying, "Those who practice the Dharma are protected by the Dharma." Another way of saying this is that those who practice in accord with nature are protected by nature. Those who practice the truth are in turn protected by the truth.

May you all be protected by your nature.

A "charioteer" I call the one
Who keeps in check
The unsteady chariot of arisen anger.
Others merely hold the reins.

—*Dhammapada 222*

WORKING WITH ANGER

A tension frequently arises between Buddhist teachings and Western attitudes towards anger. When I give a talk on anger—describing how to work with it, how to not be controlled by it, and how to let go of it—inevitably someone will say, "I don't think that anger is bad or that we need to get rid of it. It can play a useful role in our lives." These comments may come from the assumption that the English use of the word "anger" is the same as the Buddhist use. Often, they are referring to somewhat different experiences.

The Buddhist word *dosa*, usually translated as anger, might more accurately be translated as "hostility," provided we recognize that hostility can be present in emotions ranging from minor aversion to full-blown rage. While the English word anger can include hostility, it doesn't have to. The West has a long tradition of accepting certain forms of non-hostile anger as appropriate—for example, a forceful protest against injustice.

Dosa burns the one who is angry. Classic Buddhist teachings liken being angry to holding a red-hot piece of coal. For Buddhists, acting on *dosa* is never justified; *dosa* is a form of suffering that Buddhist practice is designed to alleviate.

One ancient Buddhist text likens *dosa* to "urine mixed with poison." In ancient India, urine was considered to have medicinal properties; it was unpleasant but beneficial. However, when urine is mixed with poison, the unpleasant medicine becomes harmful. At times a forceful "No!" is required of us even though it may be unpleasant. But an energized "no" mixed with hostility is like mixing urine with poison.

Dosa holds people out of our hearts, away from our kindness and care. We don't necessarily need to avoid anger, but we do need to guard ourselves from locking others out of our hearts.

How can we work with this difficult emotion?

Meditation can be very helpful. In it we can experience our anger without inhibitions, judgments, or interpretations. To discover a capacity for witnessing anger without either pushing it away or engaging with it can be a great relief. In fact, meditation may well be the safest place to be angry, to learn to let it flow through us freely, without either condemnation or approval.

With non-reactive mindfulness as the foundation, we can investigate anger deeply through the body, emotions and thoughts. Anger can open us to a world of self-discovery.

Anger tends to be directed outward toward an object, toward other people, events, or even parts of ourselves. In mindfulness meditation, we turn the mind away from the object of anger and focus it inwardly to study the source of the anger and the subjective experience of being angry.

We can investigate anger through the sensations of the body. The direct experience of anger may result in sensations of heat, tightness, pulsation or contraction. The breathing may become heavy or rapid, and the heartbeat strong. Because these sensations are direct and immediate, bringing attention to them helps lessen the preoccupation with the object of the anger and with the story of why we are angry. This in turn, helps us to be more fully present for the anger in and of itself.

Turning our attention away from the object of our anger is important because, while the conditions giving rise to anger may be varied, the *direct* causes of hostile anger are found within the person who is angry. These causes include aversion, grasping, resentment, fear, defensiveness, and other reactions that may be unnecessary and are often the source of the greatest pain in a difficult situation. A traditional folk saying states, "An enemy can hurt you physically; but if the enemy wants to hurt your heart, you have to help by getting angry."

Hostile anger seems to have its roots in recoiling from our own pain. We may react to our own sadness, loneliness, fear, disappointment or hurt by directing anger outwards rather than experiencing these feelings. Learning to explore our pain honestly and non-reactively through the mental events and bodily sensations is an important step to freedom.

In my own life, I've learned that my anger tends to have two primary causes: fear and hurt. When I get angry, if it seems appropriate, I remove myself from the situation and try to be mindful of what is going on inside. If I can find the fear or the hurt underlying the anger, then (if possible) I'll go back into the situation and speak from the perspective of being hurt or afraid.

Conversations tend to be more helpful when I do this, partly because I am not assigning blame. This often lessens the other person's defensiveness or reactivity. He or she may even be more inclined to see his or her own responsibility.

Anger is always a signal. Mindfulness helps reveal what it signals. Sometimes the signal tells us that something in the external world needs to be addressed, sometimes that something is off internally. If nothing else, anger is a signal that someone is suffering. Probably it is you. Sit still in the midst of your anger and find your freedom from that suffering.

For one who is awake, non-perplexed,
   Whose mind is uncontaminated,
And who has abandoned both good deeds and bad,
   Fear does not exist.

                              —*Dhammapada 39*

When we engage in a spiritual practice, we can expect to discover the degree to which apprehension and fear are not only present, but at times run our lives. Much of our life is motivated by feelings of fear, apprehension, anxiety, dread, worry, or distrust, probably more than most of us realize. Fear is at the root of many types of psychological suffering, and an important part of mindfulness practice is to study it—to understand and accept it enough that we do not live under its influence.

It can be obvious that fear is debilitating when it inhibits us from engaging in normal activity. Also debilitating can be our efforts to avoid, ignore, or resist fear. We would do well to follow the Buddha's example. Before he became a Buddha, he included fear as part of his practice whenever it arose. We can do the same. We can learn to practice with our fear and so overcome at least its debilitating influence if not the fear itself.

Mindfulness of fear begins by getting to know its immediate

and obvious manifestation. We don't psychoanalyze it, try to fig-ure out what the layers are, or what lies at its root. Our job as mindfulness practitioners is to meet, directly and without com-plications, what is in front of us.

We react to our experience in many stages or generations. Say, for example, I'm afraid of failure, and then I'm afraid of my fear, and then I'm angry with myself because I'm afraid of my fear. Then I become ashamed of myself because I'm angry, and then I feel guilty because I should know better. And so on.

Often we live our lives in the fourteenth or fifteenth—maybe even the one hundred fifteenth—generation of reactivity to our primary experience. Our task in mindfulness practice is to wake up where we are, even if it is at the one hundred fifteenth gener-ation, rather than to be further upset with ourselves. We try to accept the latest generation; to not complicate it any further, to have a direct straightforward relationship with whatever is pres-ent. As mindfulness becomes stronger, we wake up earlier and earlier, until eventually we awaken at the first generation.

When working with fear in meditation, it is not necessary to always confront the fear directly, especially if it seems over-whelming. Instead we can try to become calm in the midst of it. One of the classic ways of becoming calm is breathing mindful-ly. The more fully the mind engages with the breath, the less it will be engaged with the fear, and so the fear loses some of its power.

When we have cultivated enough calmness so that we don't feel like we are in the grip of the fear, turning the attention to investigate the fear itself is very helpful. In mindfulness practice we do not try to deny or to get rid of our fear—that would only strengthen it. Instead we explore it, sense it, and become connoisseurs of it. In doing so we become less troubled by it. When we are less troubled by it, it is less likely to trigger other emotions such as anger, embarrassment, guilt, discouragement, or further fear. By observing the thoughts or bodily sensations that might be present, we step outside of the domain of the fear, and our identification with it lessens.

One of the primary ways to investigate fear is to feel it in the body. There might be sensations of butterflies, tightening or clenching in the stomach. There might be a sense of painful vulnerability. If the fear is quite strong, it can be difficult to be with the sensations directly. In that case, breathe with and through the discomfort, as though the breath were a massage. Breathing with the sensations can allow us to move through the fear without being caught by it.

If we have enough stability in our meditation, focusing directly on the bodily sensations associated with the fear can be very helpful. Anchoring the attention on the strongest sensations that manifest the fear helps us to disengage from the ideas and stories which activate fear. Most of the time during meditation, these stories are irrelevant to what is happening in the present moment. Holding the bodily sensations of fear in awareness helps to make room for the experience, which allows the bodily sensations to move through us. Much of the tension, tightness and constriction will begin to unravel as they are held with gentle awareness.

The fear that many people in our culture experience often has little to do with imminent danger. Instead it frequently results from an idea, an imagination of what will happen in the future. This imagination fuels the fear, worry or anxiety. We can use mindfulness practice to start learning to pay attention to the patterns of thought that relate to our fears, to see some of the common themes about what we are afraid of, and also to begin to see what triggers the fear.

When we start to recognize the patterns around our fear and to see what triggers it, then we can start to ask ourselves if these suppositions are actually true. In my practice, seeing that my projections and fears about a situation were often far different from the actual outcome helped me to overcome some of my fears. For example, once I spent two days worrying about a meeting, and then the meeting was cancelled. As this sort of painful experience happened not once, but over and over again, I slowly began to realize what a waste of time worry is! As I learned that my imaginings of the future were usually not how things turned out, my belief in the accuracy of my imaginings decreased. Certain kinds of wisdom arise only through seeing something happen repeatedly. Often we have to become very familiar with something in order to be free of it. I found this to be the case with worry.

Another way to practice with fear is to look at the beliefs that support it. Even if we know what we are afraid of, we often don't clearly see the beliefs that contribute to the fear. For example, you might know that you chronically worry about what people think about you, but not see the belief that you need to be and act a certain way in order to be accepted by others. Or perhaps you don't see the belief that we are only validated through the eyes of others. The act of looking for these beliefs and then questioning them can begin to take some of their power away.

The Buddha also taught loving-kindness practice as an antidote to fear. If you have difficulty being mindfully present with fear, you might switch to loving-kindness meditation for a while as a way of finding some spaciousness and calm. Then go back and investigate the fear.

In meditation and in mindfulness practice, we are learning to replace fear with trust, not as an ideal or abstraction, but as a sense of self-confidence that arises from coming to know fear well. Many people have a fear of fear, a tremendous aversion to it, and don't allow themselves to enter into it fully. If we simply allow ourselves to fully experience our fear, eventually we learn that we can do so without being overwhelmed by it. Trust develops, not from willing ourselves to trust, but from discovering for ourselves that we can be present for our experience and not overwhelmed by it.

Many of us have been convinced—by our society, by our own experiences in life, and by our own logic—that we cannot trust our own natural state of being. We turn away from ourselves and our experiences. In mindfulness practice we are learning not to destroy or control our feelings, but to discover them and be present with them. We begin to see how they work when we enter fully into them and give them room. We begin to see how we create our emotional lives and reactions.

In this process, we learn to trust awareness and direct presence more and more deeply. As we explore the layers of our fear, our trust expands into wider and wider circles of who we are. The process of awakening can be understood as ever-widening circles of trust. Awakening occurs when trust becomes all pervasive.

We can learn to trust awareness, to trust being alive, without props, crutches, views or opinions. In the Buddhist tradition, such people are known as dispellers of fear. They give the gift of fearlessness. Fearlessness is not necessarily the absence of fear. It is a positive quality that can exist side by side with fear, overcoming the limitations arising out of fear. Such fearlessness can be a profound gift to the people around us. In developing the capacity to be fearless, we do it not only for ourselves, but for others as well.

May all beings be happy.
May they live in safety and joy.
All living beings,
Whether weak or strong,
Tall, stout, average or short,
Seen or unseen, near or distant,
Born or to be born,
May they all be happy.

—*from the Metta Sutta*
Sutta Nipata I.8

Metta, or loving-kindness, is one of the most important Buddhist practices. Most simply, *metta* is the heartfelt wish for the well-being of oneself and others. When describing *metta*, the Buddha used the analogy of the care a mother gives her only child. Loving-kindness is closely related to the softening of the heart that allows us to feel empathy with the happiness and sorrow of the world.

Loving-kindness is also understood as the innate friendliness of an open heart. Its close connection to friendship is reflected in its similarity to the Pali word for friend, *mitta*. However, *metta* is more than conventional friendship, for it includes being open-hearted even toward one's enemies, cultivated perhaps from empathy or from insight into our shared humanity.

Metta practice is the cultivation of our capacity for loving-kindness. It does not involve either positive thinking or the imposition of an artificial positive attitude. There is no need to feel loving or kind during *metta* practice. Rather, we meditate on our intentions, however weak or strong they may be. At its heart, loving-kindness practice involves giving expression to our wishes for the well-being and happiness of ourselves or others.

In *metta* practice we water the seeds of our good intentions. When we water wholesome intentions instead of expressing unwholesome ones, we develop those wholesome tendencies within us. If these seeds are never watered they won't grow. When watered by regular practice they grow, sometimes in unexpected fashions. We may find that loving-kindness becomes the operating motivation in a situation that previously triggered anger or fear.

Recognizing and expressing goodwill have a softening effect on our hearts. At times this evokes feelings of love, tenderness, and warmth. At other times this softening of the heart can expose difficult or painful buried emotions. Allowing all these emotions to surface in their own time is one function of loving-kindness practice.

When we find difficulty in relating to others and ourselves with intentions of kindness, the practice of *metta* can provide a useful reference point to help us see what we are in fact feeling. The absence of loving-kindness can be an important cue, not to provoke self-criticism, but to remind us to slow down and pay more careful attention to what is actually happening.

The practices of mindfulness and loving-kindness support one another. *Metta* practice complements mindfulness by encouraging an attitude of friendliness toward our experience regardless of how difficult it may be. Mindfulness complements loving-kindness by guarding it from becoming partial or sentimental.

Metta can foster a closeness in our relationships to others; mindfulness can help keep us balanced in those relationships. Mindfulness can bring freedom; loving-kindness ensures that our path to freedom is not aloof from others.

As a mother watches over her child,
Willing to risk her own life to protect her only child,
So with a boundless heart, should one cherish all living beings,
Suffusing the whole world with unobstructed loving-kindness.

Standing or walking, sitting or lying down,
During all one's waking hours
May one remain mindful of this heart, and this way of living
That is the best in the world.

—*from the Metta Sutta*
Sutta Nipata I.8

BRIEF INSTRUCTIONS FOR LOVING-KINDNESS MEDITATION

To practice loving-kindness meditation, sit in a comfortable and relaxed manner. Take two or three deep breaths with slow, long and complete exhalations. Let go of any concerns or preoccupations. For a few minutes, feel or imagine the breath moving through the center of your chest—in the area of your heart

Metta is first practiced toward oneself, since we often have difficulty loving others without first loving ourselves. Sitting quietly, mentally repeat, slowly and steadily, the following or similar phrases:

May I be happy.
May I be well.
May I be safe.
May I be peaceful and at ease.

While you say these phrases, allow yourself to sink into the intentions they express. Loving-kindness meditation consists primarily of connecting to the intention of wishing ourselves or others happiness. However, if feelings of warmth, friendliness, or

85

love arise in the body or mind, connect to them, allowing them to grow as you repeat the phrases. As an aid to the meditation, you might hold an image of yourself in your mind's eye. This helps reinforce the intentions expressed in the phrases.

After a period of directing loving-kindness toward yourself, bring to mind a friend or someone in your life who has deeply cared for you. Then slowly repeat phrases of loving-kindness toward them:

> *May you be happy.*
> *May you be well.*
> *May you be safe.*
> *May you be peaceful and at ease*

As you say these phrases, again sink into their intention or heartfelt meaning. And, if any feelings of loving-kindness arise, connect the feelings with the phrases so that the feelings may become stronger as you repeat the words.

As you continue the meditation, you can bring to mind other friends, neighbors, acquaintances, strangers, animals, and finally people with whom you have difficulty. You can either use the same phrases, repeating them again and again, or make up phrases that better represent the loving-kindness you feel toward these beings.

In addition to simple and perhaps personal and creative forms of *metta* practice, there is a classic and systematic approach to *metta* as an intensive meditation practice. Because the classic meditation is fairly elaborate, it is usually undertaken during periods of intensive *metta* practice on retreat.

Sometimes during loving-kindness meditation, seemingly opposite feelings such as anger, grief, or sadness may arise. Take these to be signs that your heart is softening, revealing what is held there. You can either shift to mindfulness practice or you can—with whatever patience, acceptance, and kindness you can muster for such feelings—direct loving-kindness toward them. Above all, remember that there is no need to judge yourself for having these feelings.

As you become familiar with loving-kindness practice during meditation, you can also begin to use it in your daily life. While in your car, or at work, or in public anywhere, privately practice *metta* toward those around you. There can be a great delight in establishing a heartfelt connection to all those we encounter, friends and strangers alike.

Searching all directions
with one's awareness,
one finds no one dearer
than oneself.
In the same way, others
are fiercely dear to themselves.
So one should not hurt others
if one loves oneself.

—*Samyutta Nikaya 3.8*

COMPASSION:
MEETING SUFFERING WITHOUT RESISTANCE

Compassion is one of the central values and ideals of Buddhist practice. However, seeing it as an ideal makes it easy to overlook the difficult circumstances in which it arises. Compassion doesn't come about in the abstract. It arises when we are in direct enough contact with actual suffering to be moved by it, whether the suffering is our own or the suffering of others.

We can meet suffering with or without resistance. To resist suffering is to meet it with fear, despair, condemnation, timidity or projection. And if we project our own problems and sorrows onto others who are suffering, not only are we in a poor position to provide help, we can easily drift into grief, pity or anxiety.

When we meet suffering without resistance, suffering does not make us a victim. Rather it can be motivating in two ways. On one hand it may ignite the wish, perhaps even the passion, for spiritual practice to resolve the roots of suffering within ourselves. This means having the motivation to clarify our resistances, clingings, and fears as well as our joys and strengths. On the other hand, our contact with suffering may awaken the compassionate wish to alleviate that suffering. The Buddhist word for compassion, *karuna*, means more than just empathy; it includes the desire and motivation to end suffering. Even when we do not have the ability to help directly, such caring can offer comfort.

As an ideal, *karuna* means being present for suffering without denial, defensiveness or aversion. However, in the actual messiness of our life, we may simply learn to be compassionate toward our own tendencies of denial, defensiveness and aversion, and the pain from which these are born. The willingness to sit in the midst of our life is what begins the process of dissolving the places of tension, fear, and the like. With honest presence and compassion, resentment dissolves into forgiveness, hatred into friendliness, and anger into kindness. However, when we are lost in our busyness, ambitions, escapes, or fantasies, compassion has no chance to arise.

As we become more accepting of ourselves and of our own suffering, we begin to feel more fully the suffering of others. Mindfulness practice helps connect us with others as equals. This in turn guards us from mistaking sentimental pity—feeling sorry for others while feeling separate—for compassion.

Suffering is a universal human experience; meeting it with compassion is one of the noblest capacities we have as humans.

Don't disregard merit, thinking,
"It won't come back to me!"
With dripping drops of water
Even a water jug is filled.
With trivial acts repeated
A wise one is filled with merit.

—*Dhammapada 122*

PATIENCE

In our busy lives, we may overlook the value of patience in a quest for accomplishment, efficiency and fulfillment. When we recognize that clear-seeing, peace, compassion and love are quite different from, even incompatible with, compulsive behavior and reactions, the value of patience becomes apparent. Patience entails choosing not to respond reactively. It provides tremendous support for mindfulness practice. Perseverance, patience under insult, and acceptance of truth are three traditional facets of patience that give strength to mindfulness.

The patience of *perseverance*, through a gentle and steady effort, keeps us from succumbing to doubt, discouragement and fear. When progress in practice does not meet our expectations, we can easily become discouraged. For example, practice often gives rise to pleasant states; if we assume we can sustain them at will, the reality of change can be quite unpleasant. Or, we may expect practice to develop linearly, with increasing concentration and peace, or steadily decreasing suffering. In fact, a period of ease in practice might well provide the inner strength and trust to confront long-ignored difficulties. Practice is much easier to sustain over the long term if we realize that it doesn't always unfold in an even, expected way.

Perseverance can also be important when spiritual practice *does* meet our expectations. When things are going well, we may become complacent. In the presence of happiness or ease, we might forget to maintain a steady dedication to practice.

A gentle perseverance allows us to practice unhindered by both the difficulties and rewards we experience. It is key to letting mindfulness practice sink deep into the marrow of our bones.

Patience under insult means not succumbing to anger, aggression or despair when threatened. Instead, it means being mindful of our reactions and emotional responses, and perhaps finding wiser ways to respond.

Pausing, even for a moment, before responding to a difficult situation is a powerful form of patience. A pause may give us a better understanding of the situation and our intentions within it. Sometimes, a pause allows for something wonderful and unexpected to arise, something that would not have happened had we rushed in to react or control.

Sometimes people find patience by changing their point of reference for understanding a challenging situation. Our understanding is often self-centered; other perspectives may be equally, if not more, appropriate. During the civil rights movement, for example, many people endured a tremendous amount of physical, mental and emotional insult by understanding its role in a larger context than their own individual suffering. Struggling for civil rights gave their suffering a purpose that transformed the whole country.

The third form of patience is *acceptance of truth*. This means the willingness to see deeply, without resistance, the truth of the moment and the truth of the deepest levels of reality. This includes living in accord with the insight that at our core there is no self to build up, hang on to, or defend. Seeing the luminous emptiness at the center of all things means that we can begin to let go of grasping to a self-conscious and fixed idea of who we are. This requires a kind of patience, because deep spiritual insight is an insult to the ego. Many people orient their lives around a limited view of themselves; it can be quite frightening to let this view go. The patient acceptance of truth that allows us to let go is a personal strength developed together with the strengths of virtue, discernment, wisdom, resolve and loving-kindness.

The ultimate perfection of patience does not come from endurance or a re-evaluation of a situation. Rather it comes from the absence of our habitual, automatic triggers and reactive hooks to the challenges of life. Fully mature, patience is effortless. It is not a doing at all.

The *Brahmana Samyutta* in the *Samyutta Nikaya* tells the story of an angry man who insulted the Buddha. The Buddha simply asked the man if people ever visited him in his home. Surprised at the change of topic, the man answered yes. The Buddha then asked if he ever offered to feed his guests. When the man replied yes again, the Buddha asked what would happen if they refused to accept the food? Who would the food belong to then? The man said that, of course, it would still belong to him. The Buddha then calmly and, I imagine, kindly said, "In the same way, I do not accept your insults. They remain with you."

Because the ultimate patience is effortless, perhaps the opposite of impatience is not patience but rather contentment. By not chasing after the whims of the ego, we have the chance to discover a deep contentment that manifests in our life as great patience.

Wisdom arises from practice;
  Without practice it is lost.
Knowing these two ways of gain and loss,
  Conduct yourself so that wisdom grows.
                                    —*Dhammapada 282*

THE PERFECTION OF WISDOM

Buddhism is sometimes known as a wisdom tradition: the practice of awakening is supported by and expressed in a deep understanding of life. Wisdom is also one of the ten qualities or "perfections" developed in Buddhist practice.

The Buddhist tradition distinguishes three kinds of wisdom, each of which has a place in the spiritual life: wisdom acquired through learning, reflection, and developing meditation.

People sometimes hold wisdom in opposition to knowledge, undervaluing study. But in Buddhism, the knowledge that comes from learning is appreciated as a form of wisdom. Studying the teachings is a valuable foundation for the practice. Studying includes reading the words of Buddhist and other spiritual teachers. It can include classes. Traditionally it also includes memorization of Buddhist writings. I sometimes ask practitioners to memorize short texts or passages, and wonderful things can occur. A memorized passage seems to be processed within us in subtle and varied ways apart from our intellectual understanding. A line or passage will suddenly appear in the mind at an opportune time, providing a new perspective on the teachings or on the words' application in our lives.

The second form of wisdom is reflective wisdom: using our powers of reflection to think about important themes in our lives. This includes discussions with friends, fellow practitioners, and teachers. Sometimes people think that mindfulness is in opposition to reflection—i.e., because mindfulness is non-discursive, discursive activity must somehow be unspiritual. The tradition, however, doesn't see reflection and mindfulness as opposed. Each one has its importance.

Any topic can be the subject of careful reflection. In Buddhist practice it is considered valuable to reflect upon, digest, and challenge such teachings as the Four Noble Truths, the Eightfold Path, impermanence, non-self, karma, and dependent co-arising. An important traditional subject of reflection is death. There is a saying that age brings wisdom. This wisdom may come from increased life experience, but perhaps even more so from a sense of the proximity of death. When the actuality of death becomes clear to us, it can be a source of wisdom. It may clarify our intentions and priorities. Rather than a morbid concern, reflecting on death can help us live our life mindfully, appreciating what is most important.

The third kind of wisdom is that of developing meditation. This is the understanding that arises from developing the qualities of mind—such as mindfulness—that allow us to see deeply into the nature of our experience. Most people take their experience for granted, relating only to surface appearances. We tend not to question the very nature of the experience itself, and miss an opportunity to see more deeply.

As the non-discursive investigation of mindfulness becomes stronger, our vision is less and less filtered through our ideas. We begin to see things more clearly for what they are. As mindfulness becomes more penetrating, we see the three universal characteristics of experience: all experiences are impermanent, none are satisfactory refuges of lasting happiness, and no experience or thing known through awareness can qualify as a stable self.

As we meet these characteristics directly, wisdom grows. We begin to understand the suffering that comes from resisting the constant flux of experience. We begin to see that mindfulness can lead us to a happiness that is not dependent on our experience. And we gain ease in our lives. We find a place of freedom with no self to defend or bolster. We can see our shortcomings and our pain without their limiting us, without believing that they define who we are.

The perfection of wisdom, of insight, comes when the heart and mind neither cling to nor resist anything. Seeing the three characteristics is a powerful step to this perfection. It leads to an awareness that doesn't appropriate, doesn't fixate on our experiences. The mind and heart allow experiences to reside and pass through, as they are. From this place, we can more wisely decide how to act, when to take a stand, and how to say what needs to be said. The art of liberation is learning how to do what we have to in life, without the mind or heart becoming contracted or tense. In *Ash Wednesday*, T. S. Eliot expresses this wisdom beautifully: "Teach us to care and not to care." To care and not to care at the same time. It's not one or the other.

More often than we realize, we have an alternative to holding things in opposition. Study, reflection and developing meditation strengthen the practice of mindfulness. They help us toward liberation, and bring harmony to our lives and the lives of others.

The restless, agitated mind
Hard to protect, hard to control,
The sage makes straight
As a fletcher, the shaft of an arrow.

—*Dhammapada 33*

CONCENTRATION

Just as a rudder can hold a ship steady on its course, concentration offers stability and steadfastness to the practice of mindfulness. Indeed, concentration is so important in Buddhist practice that it is often considered an equal partner to mindfulness. Without the stabilizing force of concentration, we cannot sustain mindful attention on the things that are most important to us, including meditation. We easily become preoccupied instead of awake.

We can more easily develop concentration if we understand its value, and appreciate that focusing mindfully on something like our breathing is actually useful. To someone unfamiliar with the practice of concentration, focusing on something unconnected to our major concerns can seem illogical and counter-intuitive. But twenty or thirty minutes spent attending to the breath gives most people a tangible appreciation for the power of concentration.

A mind without concentration is distractible and easily lost in preoccupations. The mind can be so "distracted by distractions it does not even know it is distracted," so tight around preoccupations that it's difficult to see beyond the tightness.

The concerns of our lives can preoccupy us very powerfully— so much so that we often do not notice that we may have some choice about the ways we understand and relate to them. Sometimes we assume that if we can only find the right understanding of a problem, we will be able to resolve it. We think that the only way of relating to our thoughts and concerns is in the very world of our thoughts and concerns itself.

We are as if in the middle of a maze in which the walls are just a little higher than our eyebrows. We walk around looking for the way out, bumping into walls, going down dead ends. Our emotions swing between hope and discouragement, unfounded confidence and fear. Stuck in the maze, we may feel an urgent need to get out, and yet it seems so difficult. But if we simply stood on our tiptoes and looked over the walls, from a higher vantage point we would easily see the way out.

Our world of thoughts and concerns can be like a maze; we don't realize that all we have to do is "stand on our toes" to get a broader view. From a higher vantage point, our problems may appear very different. We may not be able to change the problem itself, but through mindfulness supported by concentration we may be able to shift our perspective and radically change the way we relate to the situation.

Concentration brings calm, which can open the possibilities of new relationships toward our concerns. Most of us know that a calm mind allows us to see and think more clearly. But it can also help us to understand our concerns in a completely new way.

It allows us to step outside of the maze-like context of the concerns themselves. Such problems as interpersonal relationships, work, health, and personal identity can be seen in the light of our deepest integrity and values rather than through fears, desires, and popular, superficial values.

In a more profound sense, the over-arching perspective of calm awareness may show us that having problems may be completely acceptable. We realize that our ability to be whole and complete is not compromised by the problem. In fact, our wholeness actually includes the problem. This does not mean we become complacent, but that our attempts to fix our problems need not be colored by a sense of insufficiency, inadequacy, or neediness.

When we are caught by a problem, a great deal of energy can be poured into our preoccupation. With concentration practice, we consciously put our energy into staying present and awake to something wholesome.

A classic focus for developing concentration is the breath. By staying with the breath and matter-of-factly returning to it when the mind wanders, we strengthen our concentration and weaken preoccupation. With time, the mind finds rest, openness, and calmness.

To cultivate concentration on the breath, you can explore various ways of paying attention to the breath. You can try resting your attention on the breath or floating on the sensations of breathing. Try taking an interest in each breath as if it were your first—or last. See if you can enjoy the sensual quality of breathing. Let yourself become absorbed in the breathing process. Feel devotion and love for your breathing. Discern when gentle, compassionate acceptance supports the development of concentration and when a greater firmness of purpose is more appropriate. As your ability to sustain attention on the breath strengthens, the forces of preoccupation will weaken and you will probably find yourself calmer, lighter and more spacious.

When the mind becomes quite spacious and open, we can experience difficulties without feeling that they belong to us personally. For example, seeing physical pain as "my" pain tends to trigger feelings and ideas associated with our self-concepts, while seeing it simply as pain can make bearing it much easier. Likewise with strong emotions: if we aren't preoccupied with interpretations of what the emotion says about our personal identity, our emotional lives become easier.

The most important function of concentration within mindfulness practice is to help keep our mindfulness steady and stable in the present so that we can see clearly what is actually occurring. Our present lived experience is the door to the deepest insights and awakening. Concentration keeps us in the present so mindfulness can do its work.

See the world as a bubble;
  See it as a mirage.
The King of Death does not see
  One who so regards the world.

—*Dhammapada 170*

RECEPTIVE AWARENESS

Our awareness is like the air around us: we rarely notice it. It functions in all our waking moments, and a form of awareness may even continue in sleep. Some people don't recognize the functioning of awareness because it has never been pointed out to them. Even when we know about it, we easily take it for granted and don't appreciate it fully.

Perhaps the prime reason we don't notice awareness is that we are caught up in the content of our awareness, that is, we are preoccupied with what we think, feel, and experience. Usually daily life entails negotiating our way through what awareness knows, the content of our thinking and perception. An important part of Buddhist practice entails being aware of the other half of perception, receptive awareness itself. Becoming aware of awareness itself is a capacity we all have. Meditation offers a powerful opportunity to discover and rest in a receptive mode of knowing.

Receptive awareness is very close to the idea of a witnessing consciousness. Beginners in meditation often assume that our ability to witness means that there is someone who is witnessing; a particular, unique, and lasting subject or agent within us that is the witness. We have a strong tendency to dichotomize our world, especially between the perceived and the perceiver. Similarly, we often make a distinction between the doer and the action: I'm the doer and I am doing something, I am the speaker who is speaking. Most of us consider the idea that there is a perceiver or a doer to be simple common sense. Buddhism challenges this assumption.

These dichotomies are the cornerstone of the huge edifice of self. As soon as we have a perceiver, we have a concept of self, which becomes a magnet for all sorts of culturally conditioned ideas about what a self should be like. Our sense of self can be closely and painfully related to ideas of what is worthy, what is good, and what is required from the world around us.

Emotions can arise directly from the way we conceive our "self." If our self-image is threatened, we can easily get angry or fearful. Guilt can come from relating a self-image to ideas of good and bad, right and wrong. Both praise and blame can energize us when they affect the way we define and represent ourselves. And when our sense of self is neither supported nor threatened, some people get bored—bored with the people they are with or bored with the situation.

Resting in receptive awareness is an antidote to our efforts of building and defending a self. As this capacity develops and we begin to trust it, the assumption that there is "someone who is aware" falls away. Self-consciousness falls away. Sometimes this is called an experience of non-dualistic awareness: the distinctions between self and other, inside and outside, perceiver and perceived disappear. There is no one who is aware; there is only awareness and experience happening within awareness.

Part of what we learn to do in practice is to steady our attention, to develop a simple, receptive awareness. We aren't necessarily abandoning the world of ideas or even the idea of self. Instead, we learn to hold our lives, our ideas, and ourselves lightly. We rest in a spacious and compassionate sphere of awareness that knows but is not attached. In this way our response to life can arise from our direct experience rather than from our abstract ideas and attachments.

Let go of what's to the front,
Let go of what's behind,
And let go of what's between!
Gone beyond becoming
With the mind released of everything
You do not again undergo birth-and-aging.
—Dhammapada 348

AWAKENING—AWARENESS SET FREE

One of the most challenging aspects of Buddhism is its emphasis on the experience of *Nibbana/Nirvana*—a way of knowing that remains unswayed by the shifting conditions of life. Mindfulness practice helps us to connect to our lives honestly and intimately. But beyond that, mindfulness opens the possibility of an awareness that clings to or resists nothing. To experience this possibility fully is sometimes called Awakening.

Our awareness is often caught up with and controlled by our many pre-occupations with the conditions of life—for example, with our health, appearances, social relationships, security, employment, recreational opportunities, and opinions. However, life offers no guarantee that we can completely control these conditions, and if our happiness is dependent on how these are, then we are setting ourselves up for unhappiness. Occasionally being stripped of our control of these conditions can be a blessing, as we are challenged to discover a depth of experience that is independent of such things.

Buddhism points to Awakening to help us discover aspects of life that are usually overlooked, especially unconditioned awareness and unbounded love. To do Buddhist practice is to discover, appreciate, and strengthen the innate awareness that is independent of gain and loss, praise and blame, pleasure and pain, success and failure. Negotiating life's conditions with grace and generosity is easier when we have tasted an awareness that does not cling to those conditions.

We know that space in and of itself is difficult to describe, yet it can be described through reference to the objects that delimit it. Awakening is even more difficult to describe, as it has no direct relationship to the subjective and objective experiences of the world. Awakened awareness has a clarity much like that of a window clean enough to be unnoticed as we look through it. As it is absent of greed, hatred and fear, it is closely akin to an all-encompassing trust in awareness. As it is free from all forms of conflict, Awakened awareness is sometimes characterized as peaceful. As it is without clinging, it is celebrated as the portal of compassion.

To take the path of Awakening is to be dedicated to mindfulness and investigation no matter what happens or what else we choose to do. It is to take refuge in mindfulness regardless of whether or not we are healthy, employed, wealthy, homeless, in a relationship, and so on. To practice attentiveness regardless of circumstances is to cultivate an open-mindedness in all situations and to notice compassionately and non-judgmentally where attention is caught or fixated.

When mindfulness matures enough that we are refreshed by Awakening, then we no longer take the conditioned world to be the center of our universe. The taste of the unconditioned offers a kind of Copernican revolution in awareness. This will naturally cool the fevers of the many manifestations of greed, hatred and delusion, and the compassionate heart will grow bigger—seemingly to include everything within itself.

Happy is the arising of Buddhas;
  Happy is the teaching of the Good Dharma;
Happy is the harmony of the Sangha;
  Happy is the austerity of those in harmony
                    —*Dhammapada 194*

TAKING REFUGE

As our meditation and mindfulness practice develop, we often discover increasing levels of trust in a personal capacity for openness and wisdom. This in turn gives rise to an increasing appreciation and even a sense of devotion to those people and teachings supporting that inner trust. In the Buddhist tradition, those people and teachings are represented by the "Three Jewels": the Buddha, the Dharma, and the Sangha. "Taking refuge" is consciously choosing to be supported and inspired by these Three Jewels.

To take refuge in the Buddha is to take refuge in wisdom and clarity. Not only does the Buddha exemplify a person who has traversed the path to freedom, he also personifies the full potential for awakening and compassion found in each of us.

To take refuge in the Dharma is, in part, to take refuge in the teachings and practices taught by the Buddha. However, more deeply, the Dharma is the marvelous and immediate awareness unobscured by our greed, hatred and delusion.

Most generally, to take refuge in the Sangha is to take refuge in the community of people who share in Buddhist practice. It can be inspiring to know that others are dedicated to living the Buddha's teachings through their ethics, mindfulness and compassion. More specifically and traditionally, taking refuge in the Sangha refers to taking refuge with the community of people who have tasted liberation—the awakening of the Buddha. To have the example and guidance of such people can be phenomenally encouraging.

Taking refuge is one of the most common rituals a lay practitioner performs in Theravada Buddhism. While it is done as a matter of course at ceremonies, during retreats, and when visiting a temple, it can be a pivotal moment when, for the first time, one takes refuge with the conscious intent of orienting one's life in accordance to one's deepest values and aspirations. Relating our practice to the Buddha, Dharma and Sangha helps ensure that our practice is not limited to intellectual concerns or issues of personal therapy. It helps solidify a wide foundation of trust and respect from which the entire practice can grow.

Do not associate with evil friends.
Do not associate with wicked people.
Associate with virtuous friends.

—*Dhammapada 78*

THE JEWEL OF THE SANGHA

Buddhist practice is supported and nourished by a community of fellow practitioners. This idea is embedded in the notion that Sangha is one of the Three Jewels, which give strength to a person's practice. While the Buddha, the Dharma, and the Sangha can be equally important as supports and refuges, the first two Jewels are more often emphasized in American Buddhist circles. People tend to be much more interested in Awakening, the practice, and the teachings than in the important role that community has in a life of practice.

It has taken some thirty years to establish the practice and teachings of *Vipassana* in the West. I feel that one of the next important developments for the American *Vipassana* movement is a stronger sense of community. We should not overemphasize it, but bring it into balance with the Buddha and Dharma. Like the three legs of a tripod, each one is needed.

Practicing alone can be very difficult. Spiritual practice often changes our values and priorities. The values of contentment, peace, generosity, love and compassion that often result from the practice can be in conflict with the values of consumerism, ambition, selfishness and insensitivity found in much of our popular culture. A community of practitioners offers mutual support for living by the alternative, spiritual values.

Also, spiritual practice in a community means that the community becomes a mirror for us, as we understand ourselves better through our relationships with other practitioners. My first motivation to live in a Buddhist community was to benefit from this mirroring, especially by more senior practitioners. The practitioners didn't support or participate in many of the ego trips and emotional reactivity that I acted on, whereas many of my friends did. And because they didn't participate I could more clearly see what I was doing.

My early years of practicing within a Buddhist community were also valuable because I was given frequent examples of people expressing compassion and kindness. Such examples were inspiring, practical lessons teaching me how I might respond in the same way.

Of course, other communities besides Buddhist ones can provide helpful mirroring and modeling. However, there is a dedication that a Buddhist community tries to live by that may well be different than most other groups. A Sangha is a place where anyone can come and practice. If we end up in conflict with someone or we don't like what they have said or done, we don't banish that person from the community. Rather we bring mindful investigation to the conflict. We try to notice any attachments, fears, projections, and confusions. We look for opportunities for reconciliation, and for wise ways of respecting one another and making room for differences. This dedication of inclusion means that a Sangha is, or aims to be, a safe place for people to be themselves, which is a prerequisite for the deepest work of Buddhist practice.

For the same reason, a Sangha is also a safe place to experiment with new ways of being. As practice relaxes our insecurities and automatic patterns of behavior, a Sangha can be, for example, a place for compulsive speakers to explore speaking less, or inhibited speakers to explore new ways of speaking up.

While there can be many benefits to practicing with others, we must be aware of possible problems. As soon as a group of people gathers as a community, there is a culture, and cultures always have blind spots, or "shadows". If you avoid being involved with a community because it has a shadow, no community will ever be adequate. If you relate only to the light of a community, you are doing yourself a disservice. If you relate only to the shadow, you are also doing yourself a disservice. A function of Buddhist practice is to clarify and draw out the shadow, bringing it into balance with the light. Without honest practice, a culture's shadow can remain hidden.

For example, one of the common shadows of Buddhist communities is anger. This is in great part because Buddhists value kindness and compassion. And the more a culture values kindness and compassion, the greater the degree to which anger and hostility will be pushed into the shadows. People will be reluctant to show that side of themselves, sometimes even to themselves. The practice of mindfulness is the antidote to hidden shadows. As we become more present for our body, our feelings, and our thoughts, we will become increasingly honest about both our inner and our shared outer life.

Life is made up of encounters and we learn about ourselves in the encounters. In relation to Buddhist practice, we look at what we bring to each encounter. How do we allow other people to encounter us, and how do we encounter them? To meditate and to settle on oneself, and encounter the world from that settled place is a wonderful thing. A practice community is a place to begin learning to bring that settled place into the rest of our lives.

Attentiveness is the path to the Deathless.
Inattentiveness the path to death.
The attentive do not die,
The inattentive are as if dead.

—*Dhammapada 21*

QUESTIONING AS PRACTICE

In my first question to a Buddhist teacher I asked, "What kind of effort is needed to practice Zen meditation?" He questioned back, "Who is it that makes the effort?" His response made no sense to me; the conversation came to an immediate end. As I mulled over this exchange, I concluded that I would have to answer both my own question and his counter-question for myself. In doing so I discovered that there are certain spiritual questions that we answer only through our own direct experience.

Over the years, a series of such questions have motivated and directed my practice. A question of this kind propelled my early Zen practice: "How can I be alone in the company of others?" In other words, how can I interact socially without fear and ego? This question loomed in importance after a period of solitude in which I discovered a freedom and peace that was unsurpassed by anything I had experienced before. Rather than turning toward solitude as a solution to my difficulties in the world, the question prodded me to keep exploring and practicing in social life.

Later, another question directed my Zen practice: "How do I participate most fully with the issue at hand?" Or, how do I overcome the tendency to hold back and feel separated from whatever I am doing, whether it is breath meditation or chopping vegetables? This proved to be a very useful line of exploration, because it kept my practice focused on what was happening rather than on ideals, hopes or self-preoccupations. I didn't look to my teachers to answer these questions. Nor were these questions that called for pat answers. They were to be answered anew in each situation.

Richard Baker-Roshi, one of my first Zen teachers, encouraged his students to reflect at length on our concerns and questions until we found their "kernel." Many of us tended to conjure up long narratives from our lives and personal relationships as preludes to asking for advice. Or, we would ask abstract questions about Buddhist philosophy. As an alternative to such questions, Baker-Roshi directed us to refine the question down to the core of the identity, intention, or viewpoint upon which it rested. For example, when I was kitchen supervisor in the monastery I had difficult relationships with my crew. I didn't rush off to a teacher to describe the difficulties and ask for advice. Instead, I lingered with my inner tensions until I realized that my contribution to these tensions was a fear-driven desire to be liked by everyone, in all circumstances. Realizing this I found it more productive to come to terms with the need to be liked rather than to "fix" the external relationships. And in attempting to do so, questions eventually focused the inquiry: "Who is the self that wants to be liked?" and "Who is this self that is afraid?" At the time, I did not know how to answer. However, much like that first counter-question—"Who is it that makes the effort?"—these questions provided motivation to continue my practice.

Often, the greater the meditative stillness that holds an essential question, the more likely a resolution will well up from within. I experienced this when I faced the question of whether to begin graduate school or to enter a Buddhist monastery. When I gave mindful, non-reflective room to my inner sense of struggle and discomfort, I was surprised that a remarkably clear decision arose to enter the monastery.

Later in Burma, key questions continued to propel my practice of intensive *Vipassana* meditation. One was "What is it to be thorough in the practice?" Another was the classic, "What is the Self?"—a distilled version of "Who is it that makes the effort?" and "Who is this self that is afraid?" With wills almost of their own, these questions spurred me to keep drawing attention away from my preoccupations and back to investigation. My *Vipassana* teacher, Sayadaw U Pandita reinforced this approach. He was strict in directing his students to investigate their direct experience instead of asking abstract existential questions. He had a tremendous confidence and insistence that if we looked deeply and clearly enough we could discover whatever is needed for becoming more awake and free. The only question that seemed appropriate and universal was "What is this?" We were to cultivate an unbroken and relaxed investigation, to continue seeing ever more deeply into the particulars of the present moment's experience.

In practicing mindfulness in this way, I found it useful to turn the question, "What is this?" back toward the quality of the awareness that knows or is investigating. Such turning of attention back on itself can have a number of fruits. It can highlight any grasping, aversion, or complacency that has become mixed in with how we practice. Perhaps more profoundly, it can reveal the clearly insubstantial nature of our self-concepts, that is, of all concepts of a self, of a knower that experiences.

The ultimate value of inquiry within Buddhist practice lies with strengthening our trust, equanimity and capacity to remain open in all circumstances. And when meditative equanimity is mature, a simple question, an opening to unknown possibilities, can sometimes release the last threads that tie us to the conditioned world, moving us toward greater freedom.

One is not a Noble One
Who harms living beings.
By being harmless to all living beings
Is one called "a Noble One."

—Dhammapada 270

RESPONDING TO TRAGEDY

At the heart of Buddhism lie both realism and optimism. The realism entails an honest and unswerving recognition of the suffering and violence in our world. These existed at the time of the Buddha and they continue in our modern world. The optimism comes from recognizing the potential for alleviating suffering and violence. We can in fact remove from our hearts the toxic forces of greed, hate, and delusion. We can replace them with peace, loving-kindness, and compassion. For Buddhist practice, it is important to be both realistic and optimistic. Realism alone leads to despair. Optimism alone obscures the ground of spiritual practice.

In the face of unimaginable tragedy, violence and hate, we are called upon to honestly recognize our own fear, confusion and anger. Fear ignored produces more fear; confusion unacknowledged churns up more confusion; anger not confronted spawns further anger. To develop our mindfulness of all three is to learn

118

how to be free of their forces.

This is a slow and gradual process. But the more free we become, the more we are able to organize our lives around our best intentions. The intentions to be kind, compassionate, helpful, happy, and liberated are among the most beautiful qualities we have as humans.

These qualities are not luxuries. They are not optional. We need to be able to call upon them when we respond to the cries of the world around us. The optimism of Buddhism is that we can make a difference to the world around us. Our thoughts, words, and deeds of empathy, love and caring are the needed counter-forces to hatred, violence, and despair. Our own efforts to find inner peace, our example, can be an important force of wholesome change for people who don't know of that possibility.

The history of Buddhism offers many examples of how influential the peaceful presence of one person can be. When prince Siddhartha was dismayed by sickness, old age, and death, the sight of a peaceful renunciate inspired him with the possibilities of the spiritual quest which culminated in his awakening as the Buddha.

One of the more dramatic stories concerns the conversion of the violent king Ashoka in the third century BCE who was bent on conquering as much of India as possible. In his own words, which have survived on stones he ordered carved, he tells of being horrified at the carnage of the 100,000 deaths by which he won a battle. As he stood in grief on the battlefield, a single Buddhist monk walked by with a peace and radiance that moved the king to ask for teachings. Propelled by his own despair, the monk's serenity, and these teachings, the king renounced conquest, violence, and capital punishment. While he retained his army for defense, his efforts were redirected from war to the social and spiritual improvement of his subjects.

We can't be sure what teachings Ashoka received from the monk. The Buddha had much to say about violence and hatred; perhaps the monk repeated these verses from the Buddha:

> *Hatred never ends through hatred.*
> *By non-hatred alone does it end.*
> *This is eternal truth.*
> *Victory gives birth to hate;*
> *The defeated sleep tormented.*
> *Giving up both victory and defeat,*
> *The peaceful sleep delighted.*
>
> *All tremble at violence:*
> *All fear death.*
> *Having likened others to yourself,*
> *Don't kill or cause others to kill.*
>
> *If you surveyed the entire world*
> *You'd find no one more dear than yourself.*
> *Since each person is most dear to themselves,*
> *May those who love themselves not bring harm*
> *to anyone.*
>
> *The person who day and night*
> *Delights in harmlessness,*
> *And has loving-kindness toward all beings,*
> *Is the one who has no hate for anyone.*

In Buddhist teaching, we have available two healthy responses to the suffering of the world. One is compassion. A tremendous motivation to change the world for the better can arise out of compassion. I believe that compassion is a more effective motivation than aversion.

The other response is called *samvega*, which is the passion for practice. In our contact with suffering, we find the motivation to come to terms with our suffering, to find freedom for ourselves and others. Both responses contribute to peace.

May we all remain confident that we can make a difference.

APPENDIX

THERAVADA—THE WAY OF LIBERATION

"Theravada"—literally, The Teachings of the Elders—is an ancient Buddhist tradition that has nurtured practices and teachings of wisdom, love and liberation for over two thousand years. Liberation, the pivotal point around which the tradition revolves, is a deep seeing into and participation in the reality of "things as they are:" the world we live in when seen without the filters of greed, hatred and delusion.

With the ever-present, timeless immediacy of "things as they are" as a central reference point, the Theravada school is a fluid and varied tradition evolving in response to the particular personal, historical, and cultural circumstances of those who participate in it. Today there are over one hundred million Theravada Buddhists in Sri Lanka and Southeast Asia. Currently, the three most influential Theravada countries are Burma, Thailand and Sri Lanka, and it is from these countries that the tradition has come to the West.

Theravada Buddhism in North America

Since the 1960s, the Theravada tradition has slowly but surely found a home in North America. The two major turning points for its establishment here were the founding in 1966 of the first American Buddhist *vihara,* or monastic temple, by the Sri Lankan Buddhist community in Washington D.C., and ten years later the establishment of the *Vipassana* meditation center in Barre, Massachusetts known as the Insight Meditation Society (IMS). These two centers represent two divergent and distinct forms that Theravada Buddhism has taken in North America, namely the monastic-centered traditions and temples of the Southeast Asian immigrant groups on the one hand, and on the other the lay-centered *Vipassana* movement made up mostly of Americans of European descent. The former tend to be fairly conservative, replicating in America the various forms of Buddhism found in their native countries. The latter take a more liberal and experimental approach in finding ways Theravada Buddhism can be adapted to its lay-based American setting.

The newest form of Theravada Buddhism in the United States fits into neither of these categories. It is represented by monastic centers run and supported predominantly by Euro-Americans. An example is Abhayagiri Monastery, founded by the English monk Ajahn Amaro in 1996 in Redwood Valley, California. In addition, two other monastic centers—Metta Forest Monastery in San Diego County, California, and the Bhavana Society in High View, West Virginia—are making monastic practice available to Westerners while remaining firmly connected to their traditional Asian communities. Within these centers we could well be seeing the beginnings of an American version of Theravada monasticism.

123

Considered an ideal lifestyle for study, practice, service, and the purification of the heart, monasticism has long been a cornerstone of the Theravada tradition. However, in the twentieth century and especially in the modern West, the full range of Theravada meditation practices has been made available to the laity in an unprecedented manner. This being the case, monasticism is no longer seen as the sole carrier of the tradition, although it remains an anchor and a force of preservation.

While it is too early to tell what American Theravada Buddhism will eventually look like, it will probably exhibit at least as much diversity as it does in its Southeast Asian homeland. Perhaps it will even stretch the boundaries of what has traditionally defined it.

Basic Teachings

The Buddha encouraged people not to believe blindly but to "come and see" for themselves. Consequently, his teachings emphasize practice rather than belief or doctrine. In this spirit, many Theravadan practices are awareness practices, simple in themselves but powerful in their sustained application. In addition, the tradition also teaches practices to strengthen generosity, service, ethics, loving-kindness, compassion and right livelihood. These practices nurture the growth of an awakened and liberated heart, and help us to live wisely and compassionately.

The Theravada tradition traces its practices and teachings back to the historical Buddha. While the Buddha has been the object of great veneration, the tradition has, down through the centuries, maintained that the Buddha was human, someone who pointed out the path of practice that others may follow. The Theravada school preserves much of its collection of the Buddha's teaching in a large body of scriptures, or *Suttas*, written in Pali, the Theravada equivalent of Church Latin. These remarkable texts contain highly revered and thorough descriptions of practices, ethics, psychology, and teachings on the spiritual life. They also contain a strong warning not to give up one's own judgment in favor of the tradition and its texts, as well as a warning about simply following one's own judgment without listening to others. In the *Kalama Sutta*, the Buddha says that in deciding the truth or falsity of spiritual teachings,

> Do not go by oral tradition, by lineage of teaching, by hearsay, by a collection of scriptures, by logical reasoning, by inferential reasoning, by reflection on reasons, by the acceptance of a view after pondering it, by the seeming competence of a speaker, or because you think, "The ascetic is our teacher."

> But when you know for yourselves, "These things are unwholesome, these things are blamable; these things are censured by the wise; these things, if undertaken and practiced, lead to harm and suffering," then you should abandon them.

> But when you know for yourselves, "These things are wholesome, these things are blameless these things are praised by the wise; these things, if undertaken and practiced, lead to welfare and happiness," then you should engage in them.

A key reason for such a pragmatic criterion for determining spiritual truth or falsehood is that the Buddha was not particularly interested in establishing correct metaphysical views. He was more concerned with pointing out how to move from suffering to freedom from suffering, from suffering to liberation. Thus, the central doctrine of the Theravada tradition is found in the "Four

Noble Truths." Here the word "Truths" refers to that which is spiritually or therapeutically true and helpful. The Four Noble Truths are:

1. Suffering occurs
2. The cause of suffering is craving
3. The possibility of ending suffering exists
4. The cessation of suffering is attained through the Noble Eightfold Path

Suffering (*dukkha* in Pali) here does not refer to physical and empathetic pain, conditions that we inevitably experience. Rather, it refers to the dissatisfaction and tension we add to our lives through clinging. The first and second Noble truths are a call to recognize clearly both our suffering and the many variations of grasping and aversion that make up the clinging underlying such suffering. One reason the Theravada tradition stresses awareness practices is to help us with this recognition. The third and fourth Noble truths point to the possibility of ending such clinging-derived suffering, and of living with a liberated heart.

The experience of being free of clinging-derived suffering is known as *nibbana* (*nirvana* in Sanskrit) and is popularly called enlightenment or awakening in English. While the Theravada tradition sometimes describes *nibbana* as a form of great happiness or peace, more often it has been defined simply as the complete absence of clinging or craving. The primary reason for this negative definition is that *nibbana* is so radically different from what can be described through language that it is best not to try. Furthermore, the tradition discourages attachments to any particular ideas of enlightenment as well as to pointless philosophical or metaphysical speculation. Indeed, part of the brilliance of the Four Noble Truths is that they offer a guide to the spiritual life without the need to adhere to any dogmatic beliefs.

The Eightfold Path

The fourth Noble Truth describes the set of steps we can take to let go of clinging: the Noble Eightfold Path, namely,

1. Right Understanding
2. Right Intention
3. Right Speech
4. Right Action
5. Right Livelihood
6. Right Effort
7. Right Mindfulness
8. Right Concentration

These eight aspects to the path are often organized into three categories: wisdom, ethics and meditation (*pañña*, *sila*, and *samadhi*)

Wisdom encompasses Right Understanding and Right Intention. It begins with knowing ourselves well enough so that our motivation to practice arises from understanding how the Four Noble Truths relate to our personal situations.

Ethics encompasses Right Speech, Right Action, and Right Livelihood. Theravada Buddhism teaches that we cannot cultivate an open, trusting and non-clinging heart if our behavior is motivated by greed, hatred or delusion. A powerful way to develop and strengthen an awakened heart is to sincerely align our actions with the values of generosity, kindness, compassion, and honesty.

And finally, awareness training encompasses Right Effort, Right Mindfulness, and Right Concentration. With an effort that is neither tense nor complacent, we cultivate clarity and stability of awareness so that we can see deeply into life. This, in turn, helps facilitate the cessation of clinging.

A Gradual Training

The *suttas* frequently show the Buddha describing a gradual training to cultivate spiritual development (e.g., *Samaññaphala Sutta* in the *Digha Nikaya*, and *Ganakamoggallana Sutta* in the *Majjhima Nikaya*.) This training moves progressively from the cultivation of generosity, to ethics, to mindfulness practices, to concentration, to insight, and finally to liberation. The gradual training is an expansion of the three categories of the eight-fold path, with generosity and ethics included in *sila*, meditation practices in *samadhi*, and insight and liberation in *pañña*. While this gradual training is often presented in a linear fashion, it can also be seen in a non-linear manner as a helpful description of important elements of the spiritual path that different people develop at different times. Westerners who undertake Theravada practice often skip some of the early stages in the progression. Instead they initially focus on awareness practices, particularly mindfulness. Although there may be good reasons for this in the West, by starting with mindfulness we may be bypassing the cultivation of healthy psychological qualities of mind and heart that support its foundation. In addition, by starting with mindfulness practice, we may overlook the fact that both the awakening and awakened heart can find its expression in service to others.

Generosity

Traditional Theravada training begins with *sila* and the cultivation of generosity (*dana*). In its highest form, the practice of *dana* is neither motivated from moralistic ideas of right and wrong, nor from possible future rewards. Instead, the intention of this practice is to strengthen our ability to be sensitive and appropriately generous in all situations.

128

As generosity develops, it becomes a strength of inner openness that supports the more challenging practices of mindfulness. As the practice of generosity reveals our clinging and attachments, it helps us to appreciate how the Four Noble Truths apply to our own lives. Through generosity we connect with others, weakening any tendency toward self-centeredness or self-obsession in our spiritual lives.

Ethics

From here, the gradual training expands *sila* to include ethics, sometimes described as the cultivation of contentment, since ethical transgressions often arise out of discontentment. For a layperson, ethical training means learning to live by the five precepts:
1. To refrain from killing any living being
2. To refrain from stealing or taking what is not given
3. To refrain from sexual misconduct
4. To refrain from speaking what is not true
5. To refrain from using alcohol or drugs that cause us to be careless or heedless

The precepts are not meant as moralistic commandments, but rather as guidelines for cultivation. They are taught because they strengthen qualities of restraint, contentment, honesty, clarity and respect for life. They also create a healthy relatedness to other people and to other forms of life. We can more easily progress along the path of non-clinging when our relationships are in order.

The Theravada tradition advocates the cultivation of four warm-hearted attitudes known as the divine abidings (*brahma-viharas*): loving-kindness, compassion, sympathetic joy, and equanimity. Loving-kindness is a selfless friendliness or love that desires the good and happiness for oneself and others.

Compassion and sympathetic joy—complementary expressions of loving-kindness—involve sharing in, but in no way clinging to, the suffering and joys of others. Equanimity is an even, firm, balanced attitude toward whatever occurs, especially in situations where we cannot help others or ourselves. Theravada Buddhists commonly use these attitudes as guides for how to best live in relation to others.

Meditation

Once the foundations of generosity and ethics are established, the gradual training continues with the cultivation of meditation practices. Theravada Buddhism has a large repertoire of these, including many forms of formal sitting and walking meditation practices, as well as the development of awareness in daily activities. Meditation practices are usually divided into two categories: concentration and mindfulness.

Concentration practices emphasize the development of a stable, one-pointed, fixed focus of mind on such objects as the breath, a mantra, a visual image, or a theme like loving-kindness. States of strong concentration tend to bring about temporary but often helpful states of psychological wholeness and well-being. Loving-kindness (*metta* in Pali) is a particularly useful theme for concentration because it is the traditional antidote to all forms of aversion and self-criticism. In addition, it helps cultivate an attitude of friendliness that can support other awareness practices.

Mindfulness is the cultivation of an undistracted awareness of the unfolding of events in the present moment. In both concentration and mindfulness practices, alert awareness is stabilized in the present. With concentration practice, awareness is channeled into a controlled focus on a single object to the exclusion of all else. In contrast, mindfulness develops an inclusive, at times even choiceless awareness, noticing whatever arises predominantly in our experience. It is an accepting awareness that clarifies our feelings, thoughts, motivations, attitudes, and ways of reacting. Such awareness in turn helps us to develop compassion and equanimity, both of which support liberation.

By far the most common form of Theravada meditation practice taught in America today is mindfulness practice. In particular, it is a form of mindfulness derived from the teachings of the Buddha preserved in a scripture called *The Sutta on the Four Foundations of Mindfulness*. The four foundations—the body (which includes the breath), feelings, mental states, and *dhammas* (Sanskrit *dharmas*, the psychological processes and insights that relate to the cultivation of liberated awareness)—are the four areas of experience in which mindfulness is developed.

Insight and Liberation

With the foundations of *sila* and *samadhi*, wisdom, or *pañña*, starts to grow. The key Theravada Buddhist practice leading to both insight and liberation is mindfulness, sometimes supported by concentration exercises. Mindfulness develops the ground of trust and acceptance that enables us to open to whatever our inner and outer life might bring. While this often includes a great deal of self-knowledge, this trustful openness or non-resistance is itself the door to liberation, known in Theravada Buddhism as the cessation of all clinging. Part of the beauty of mindfulness is that each clear moment of mindfulness is itself a moment of non-clinging, and as such, is a taste of liberation.

As mindfulness becomes stronger, it directly reveals three insights that the Buddha called the three characteristics of all experience, namely that our experience is seen as impermanent, unsatisfactory, and without self.

All things are impermanent, including the way we experience ourselves and the world. Since our experiences are ever-changing, they are inherently unsatisfactory as sources of permanent security or identity. As we see that they cannot provide us with lasting satisfaction, we also realize that anything we experience does not belong to some fixed, autonomous notion of a "self"—not our thoughts, feelings or body, not even awareness itself.

Sometimes these insights trigger fear, but as our mindfulness practices mature, we realize that we can function happily in the world without needing to cling or attach to anything. So the basic insights arising out of mindfulness practice help us to cultivate trust and a healthy equanimity in the midst of our lives. As this trust grows, it weakens our need to cling. Eventually, the deepest roots of clinging—greed, hatred and delusion—release themselves and the world of liberation opens.

The fruit of this liberation is, in a sense, being in a world on to which we no longer project our clingings, fears, longings and aversions. It is to see the world of "things as they are." If the release of clinging is strong enough, we realize the direct and immediate presence of the "Deathless," a word Theravada Buddhism uses to refer to the ever-present, timeless experience of liberation.

Service

In a sense the gradual path of training ends with liberation. Liberation is the door from which compassion and wisdom flow forth without selfish clinging or identification. If our compassion has not grown, then our training is incomplete. For some, the by-product of liberation and compassion is the wish to be of service to others. This can take any one of innumerable active forms, such as aiding a neighbor in difficulty, choosing to work in a helping profession, or teaching the Dharma. Before sending his first sixty enlightened disciples out into the world to teach the Dharma, the Buddha said to them,

> My friends, I am free from all human and spiritual entanglements. And as you are likewise free of all human and spiritual entanglements, go forth into the world for the good of the many, for the happiness of the many, with compassion for the world, and for the benefit, the blessing, and the happiness of gods and humans.... Reveal the spiritual life, complete and pure in spirit and in form.

The desire to be of service can also take more passive expressions, such as living simply as a monk or nun, as an example of a life of practice. By itself, the act of Awakening is a great gift, a great act of service, because others will never again be subjected to the greed, hatred and delusion of an Awakened one. Rather they will benefit from the radiance, example and wisdom of someone set free. The gift of Awakening can be seen as bringing the spiritual path full circle, with generosity found at both the beginning and ending of the path.

Faith

A key element at every stage of the path is faith, a word that is often troublesome for Westerners. In Theravada Buddhism, faith does not mean blind belief. Rather, it describes trust or confidence in oneself, in the teachings and practices of liberation, and in the community of teachers and practitioners, both past and present. It is the kind of faith that inspires one to verify for oneself the experiential possibilities of a spiritual life.

As these possibilities become actualized, we often discover increasing levels of trust in our personal capacity for openness and wisdom. This in turn gives rise to an increasing appreciation of the people and teachings supporting this inner trust. In the Theravada tradition, these are represented by the *Three Treasures*: the Buddha; the Dharma, or teachings; and the Sangha, or the community of practitioners.

One of the most common rituals for lay practitioners in Theravada Buddhism is "Taking Refuge," consciously choosing to be supported and inspired by the Three Treasures. While "Taking Refuge" is performed as a matter of course at ceremonies, during retreats, and when visiting a temple, it can be a pivotal moment when, for the first time, one takes refuge with the conscious intent of orienting one's life in accordance with one's deepest values and aspirations. Relating our practice to the Buddha, Dharma, and Sangha helps ensure that it is not only limited to intellectual concerns, issues of personal therapy, or selfish ambitions. Taking refuge helps solidify a broad foundation of trust and respect from which true mindfulness and insight can grow.

Theravada Buddhism in Daily Life

Theravada Buddhism distinguishes between the path of liberation and the path of worldly well-being. This corresponds loosely to the Western distinction between spiritual and secular concerns. The Pali words for these two are literally the ultimate path (*lokuttara-magga*) and the mundane or worldly path (*lokiya-magga*). No absolute separation exists, and teachers vary in the degree of distinction or non-distinction they see between them. Even when a strong distinction is upheld, the spiritual and the secular paths are seen as being mutually supportive of each other.

The path of liberation is concerned with selflessness and *nibbana*, which in and of itself does not belong to the conventions, contents or conditions of the world. The path of worldly well-being is concerned with how to engage with these conventions and conditions so as to create as much personal, familial, social, economic and political health as possible.

Traditionally, *Vipassana* meditation belongs to the path of liberation. This has meant that many of those westerners who have devoted themselves to this practice both in Asia and in America have not learned much about the Theravada teachings and practices for worldly well-being. To appreciate the tradition in its full religious vitality, however, it is necessary to study both paths. This is particularly so for those who have a passion for integrating their *Vipassana* practice into their daily lives.

In a number of *suttas* popular in Southeast Asia, the Buddha speaks about how to live well in the world. The *Sigalaka Sutta* addresses the responsibilities of our social and familial roles—parent, child, spouse, teacher, student, friend, employer, employee, monastic and lay. One of the *sutta's* beautiful and challenging teachings is on earning a livelihood without creating any harm in the process:

> The wise who are trained and disciplined
> Shine out like beacon lights.
> They earn money just as a bee gathers honey
> Without harming the flower,
> And they let it grow as an anthill slowly gains in height.
> With wealth wisely gained
> They use it for the benefit of all.

Through the centuries, Theravada Buddhism has had much to say about politics. Many Southeast Asian kings have tried to live up to the list of ten virtues and duties for political leaders enumerated by the tradition: generosity, ethical conduct, self-sacrifice, honesty, gentleness, loving-kindness, non-anger, non-violence, patience, and conformity to the *Dhamma*. While those who strictly pursue the path of liberation have at times held themselves apart from worldly affairs, Theravada Buddhism as a full religious tradition has been very much engaged with political and social issues: with education, health, public works and more recently with environmental protection.

To help build healthy community, the tradition has festivals and ceremonies. It performs a range of rites of passage marking major transitions in a person's life. Although monks do not officiate in all of these, Theravada communities have rituals, practices and celebrations for birth, marriage, death, and even a ceremony of elderhood at a person's sixtieth birthday.

Students and Teachers

Theravada Buddhism teaches that friendship is an invaluable support for the spiritual life. In particular, spiritual friendships among practitioners, and between practitioners and their teachers are encouraged. Indeed, a common title for a teacher is *kalyana-mitta* or "good spiritual friend." Although teachers may give instruction, reveal delusions and attachments, open new understandings and perspectives, and provide encouragement and inspiration, their role is always limited, since we must each walk the spiritual path for ourselves. A teacher is specifically not someone to whom students renounce their own common sense or personal responsibility. Nor is it generally expected that students will devote themselves exclusively to one teacher. Practitioners commonly spend time with a variety of teachers, benefiting from each teacher's particular strengths.

Monasticism

A cornerstone of the Theravada tradition is the monastic community of monks and nuns. For much of the last two thousand years they have been the primary preservers of the Buddhist teachings and the exemplars of a life dedicated to liberation. Monasticism is often considered an ideal lifestyle for study, practice, service, and the purification of the heart. While not meant to be ascetic, the monastic life is designed to be simple, with minimal personal possessions and entanglements. As such it provides an important example of simplicity, non-possessiveness, non-harming, virtue, humility, and how to be content with little.

Not permitted to buy, cook or store their own food, Theravada monastics depend on the daily alms donations of the laity. They are thus not able to live independent of society, but must live in continual relationship to those who support them. Often this is a reciprocal relationship, with the laity supporting the monastics, and the monastics providing teaching, guidance and inspiration for the laity.

Retreats

The most popular Theravada practice in America today is mindfulness. It was introduced by young Americans who had studied in Southeast Asia, and is one of the few Asian Buddhist meditation practices popularized by Americans rather than Asian teachers. Teachers such as Joseph Goldstein, Jack Kornfield, and Sharon Salzberg (founders of IMS) streamlined the practice in order to offer an easily accessible, simple, but profound practice freed from much of its Theravada Buddhist context. As Jack Kornfield has said, "We wanted to offer the powerful practices of insight meditation, as many of our teachers did, as simply as possible without the complications of rituals, robes, chanting, and the whole religious tradition."

One of the important forms of *Vipassana* practice has been intensive meditation retreats, lasting from one day to three months. Retreats are usually conducted in silence except for instructions, interviews with the teachers, and a daily discourse or "Dharma talk" given by a teacher. A typical day begins around 5:30 a.m. and ends around 9:30 p.m. A simple daily schedule of alternating sitting and walking meditation, and including a period of work meditation, encourages the cultivation of mindfulness throughout the day.

Though American *Vipassana* students are overwhelmingly lay people, these retreats allow them to practice with the support, simplicity and focus that is usually associated with monastic life. In a sense, these retreats offer the benefits of temporary monasticism. Intensive retreat practice alternating with periods of living the practice in the world is characteristic of the American *Vipassana* movement.

Perhaps in our own lay Western way, the simplicity of retreats corresponds to the life of the Theravada forest monks who historically were often those who devoted themselves to meditation practice. Such simplicity not only supports the cultivation of intimate mindfulness, it also facilitates the discovery of the simplicity of freedom itself.

THE INSIGHT MEDITATION CENTER
OF THE MID-PENINSULA

Mission

The Insight Meditation Center (IMC) of the Mid-Peninsula is dedicated to the study and practice of Buddhist ideals—mindfulness, ethics, compassion, loving-kindness, and liberation. At the heart of all IMC activities is the practice of Insight Meditation, sometimes called mindfulness or *Vipassana* meditation. Based on a 2500-year old Buddhist teaching, this practice helps us to see more deeply and clearly into our lives. With insight, we develop ways of living more peacefully, compassionately, and wisely.

Daily practice forms the foundation of Insight Meditation practice: daily meditation practice, and the practice of mindfulness and compassion as we go about our daily lives. Buddhist tradition also emphasizes the value of one-day and longer intensive meditation retreats. IMC's mission is to stay firmly rooted in the practices of meditation and retreats. From this contemplative root, we actively seek to find ways to support practitioners in integrating and applying the spiritual life in all areas of life.

Vision

Our vision for the Insight Meditation Center of the Mid-Peninsula is to be a community-based meditation center where the practices and teachings of Insight Meditation are made available to those living urban lifestyles. IMC has four intertwining functions.

• To provide a simple and quiet environment where the contemplative life can be developed and protected amidst the complexities of city living.

• To offer teachings and practice opportunities that complement Insight Meditation in supporting a balanced spiritual life from a Buddhist perspective.

• To be a place where people can come together to cultivate and express their practice in and through their family, social, and community lives.

• To bring in a variety of visiting Buddhist teachers in order to expose our IMC community and the interested public to a range of Buddhist practices and viewpoints.

Central to forwarding this vision, IMC has purchased a building and has committed itself to expanding its programs to include regular meditation sessions, classes, group discussions, dharma talks (talks on Buddhist teachings and practice), and meetings with teachers. Periodic one and two day meditation and study retreats are offered, as well as small residential retreats at nearby centers.

History

IMC was meeting by 1986 as a sitting group organized by Howard and Ingrid Nudelman. Initially the group met at the Institute of Transpersonal Psychology in Menlo Park. From the start, the group was affiliated with Spirit Rock Meditation Center and during the first couple of years Howard Cohn, a Spirit Rock teacher, came from San Francisco to lead the sittings.

In 1988, the group moved to the First Presbyterian Church on Cowper Street in Palo Alto and most evening meetings consisted of sitting together and listening to Dharma talks on tape. In August 1990, Howard Nudelman invited Gil Fronsdal to be the regular teacher for the Monday evening meetings. Gil, who was then a teacher-in-training with Jack Kornfield, started teaching in September. At the time, 12 to 15 people attended the gatherings. The group started hosting one-day retreats in early 1991.

By 1993, the group had grown to about 40 people, and a larger meeting place was needed. In September 1993, the Monday evening sitting was moved to the Friends Meeting House on Colorado Street, Palo Alto. Attendance soon jumped to about 60 and then continued to grow steadily to about 100 who attend regularly. Monthly potluck dinners were started in the spring of 1994 on the third Monday of the month.

In response to the large gatherings on Monday evenings, in 1995 IMC began the Thursday evening meetings aimed primarily at newer practitioners. And once again in 1999, to take the pressure off the Monday gatherings and to respond to numerous requests, IMC started a Sunday morning meditation program and dharma talk in Portola Valley.

In January 1994, IMC published its first "newsletter", a

onesheet schedule of events. After a couple of issues, Bob and Bernice LaMar began publishing our regular newsletter in October 1994.

IMC put on its first residential retreat during Memorial Day weekend of 1994. This was held at Jiko-ji Zen Center off Skyline Blvd. in the mountains of Los Gatos. These weekend retreats have continued annually or bi-annually ever since. In 1999, Gil also started teaching a yearly 12 to 14 day retreat at Jiko-ji. And in 2000, IMC started inviting other teachers to lead weekend retreats.

The Children's Program was started in January 1996. This consisted of a half-hour of Dharma games and storytelling on the third Monday of each month. In the Fall of 2001 the program was expanded and moved to the last Sunday of the month. Over the years numerous other programs and events have been introduced, e.g., classes in yoga, loving-kindness and the *brahmaviharas, sutta* study, and refuge ceremony preparation. Slowly over the years there have been more community-building events—potlucks, hikes, movie nights, discussion groups, etc. In 2000, a group of IMC members organized themselves as "Dharma Friends" in order to put on a wide variety of social and practice events that help create a greater sense of community and friendship within IMC.

In the Fall of 1995 a meeting was held to consider the future of IMC. The possibility of owning our own building was discussed with much interest. In order to lay the foundation for this it was decided to incorporate as a non-profit religious organization. IMC was incorporated as a 501(c)3 in 1997.

In September of 1997 and 1998 IMC sent out its first fundraising letters to begin securing the needed funds for purchasing a building. In 1999 the group pursued purchasing the rundown and unused AME Zion Church on Ramona Street in Palo Alto. Ultimately, the church was sold to developers. However, the attempts to buy it served as a catalyst for IMC. Fund-raising increased dramatically and the Board set up numerous committees and an organizational structure that would make it possible to both buy and run a center.

In the Spring of 2000, IMC was told that two Christian ministers had a small church in Redwood City they were interested in selling to the group. In January 2001, IMC established contact with the ministers and a warm friendship ensued. On November 28, 2001 IMC bought the Church located at 1205 Hopkins. With the enthusiasm and hard work of many volunteers, the church was expeditiously converted into its current incarnation as a meditation center, and sittings and talks began there on January 6, 2002.

Having the opportunities afforded by having its own building, the programs at IMC have expanded, adding more sittings, retreats, study courses, many varied special events and other programs, as well as numerous guest teachers, including visiting monks.

Metta Sutta

To reach the state of peace
One skilled in the good
Should be
Capable and upright,
Straightforward and easy to speak to,
Gentle and not proud,
Contented and easily supported,
Living lightly and with few duties,
Wise and with senses calmed,
Not arrogant and without greed for supporters,
And should not do the least thing that the wise would critcize.

[One should reflect:]
"May all be happy and secure;
May all beings be happy at heart.
All living beings, whether weak or strong,
Tall, large, medium, or short,
Tiny or big,
Seen or unseen,
Near or distant,
Born or to be born,
May they all be happy.
Let no one deceive another
Or despise anyone anywhere;
Let no one through anger or aversion
Wish for others to suffer."

As a mother would risk her own life
To protect her child, her only child,
So toward all beings should one
Cultivate a boundless heart.
With loving-kindness for the whole world should one
Cultivate a boundless heart,
Above, below, and all around
Without obstruction, without hate and without ill-will.
Standing or walking, sitting or lying down,
Whenever one is awake,

May one stay with this recollection.
    This is called a sublime abiding, here and now.

One who is virtuous, endowed with vision,
    Not taken by views,
And having overcome all greed for sensual pleasure
    Will not be reborn again.

DONATIONS (DANA)

This book is distributed freely to all who request it.

Insight Meditation Center is committed to continuing the Buddhist tradition that all teachings be given freely. All teachings are offered with the opportunity for voluntary donations. The generosity of the community supports our teachers and pays all our Center expenses.

If you would like to support our Center with a tax-deductible contribution, please send it to:

Insight Meditation Center
1205 Hopkins Avenue
Redwood City, CA 94062

Donations may also be made online at our website:
www.insightmeditationcenter.org

"The gift of the dhamma excels all other gifts." Dhammapada

Recordings of dharma talks
by Gil Fronsdal and guest speakers at IMC
are available to listen to online or to download at
www.audiodharma.org.